THE HEART OF A MAN
PURE, HONEST, AND UNFILTERED

Dr. Monica Denise Beasley Publishing
Champaign, Illinois

Dr. Monica Beasley
Motivational Speaker · Entrepreneur ·
Singer/Songwriter · Author
Founder of Monica's Accounting & Tax Services
(MATS LLC)
Founder of Open Arms Grace Nonprofit

Copyright © 2025 by Dr. Monica Beasley

All rights reserved.

No part of this publication may be reproduced, stored in a retrieval system, or transmitted in any form or by any means—electronic, mechanical, photocopying, recording, or otherwise—without the prior written permission of the publisher, except for brief quotations used in reviews or scholarly works. Published by Dr. Monica Denise Beasley Publishing

Champaign, Illinois
ISBN (Paperback): 979-8-9991422-6-9
ISBN (eBook): 979-8-9991422-7-6

First Edition, June 2025
Printed in the United States of America
Image Credit: Joel Henry
Edited by Dr. Monica Beasley
Interior formatting by Dr. Monica Beasley

This book is a work of nonfiction. Names, places, and identifying details have been changed or omitted in some cases to protect the privacy of individuals. All stories are based on real experiences and told from the author's perspective.

For permission or inquiries, contact:
Monica Denise Beasley, Ph.D.
Monicabeasley87@gmail.com

Dedication

To the men who dare to feel, to the hearts that beat with truth, to the souls unafraid to stand bare in their vulnerability—this book is for you.

And to the one whose courage to be seen reminded me that real strength is found in softness, honesty is the bravest language, and love, when pure, is never ashamed to show itself.

May these words speak to the depths of your heart.

Acknowledgments

To God—thank You for being my constant guide, my source of strength, and the true author of every word. Your presence has been the compass leading me through every chapter of life and love.

To the man who inspired this work—you may never fully know the impact your honesty, vulnerability, and strength have had on my spirit. Thank you for showing me that a man's heart, when uncovered and pure, holds the kind of beauty the world needs more of.

To my family and friends—thank you for your love, encouragement, and prayers. Your belief in me kept me writing even when my own strength wavered.

To every reader—thank you for opening your heart to these pages. May you find healing, hope, and courage in these words, and may they remind you that the truest version of a man is the one who isn't afraid to be seen.

With love and gratitude,

Dr. Monica Beasley

Preface:

A Man's Heart is His Secret

A man's heart often lives in silence.
Behind the strength, the laughter, the responsibilities—there are thoughts he doesn't speak, feelings he doesn't show, and truths he carries alone. Society has taught him to be the provider, the protector, the one who doesn't bend or break.

This book was born from a desire to understand that space—to listen, not with judgment, but with reverence. *The Heart of a Man: Pure, Honest, and Naked* is not about exposing weakness; it's about revealing humanity. It's about giving voice to what men are often afraid to say, and celebrating the strength it takes to be fully seen.

Whether you are a man searching for language for your emotions, or someone who loves a man and wants to better understand his inner world, this book is for you. My hope is that these words open doors, spark conversations, and inspire healing in places long left unspoken.

Because when a man dares to share the secrets of his heart, he doesn't lose power—he discovers it. — **Dr. Monica Beasley**

TABLE OF CONTENTS

Dedication III
Acknowledgments IV
Preface: A Man's Heart is His Secret V
Table Of Contents VI
Introduction VII
Chapter One: Where the Wound Begins 1
Chapter Two: The Effects of A Broken Man 13
Chapter Three: What Anger Does to The Soul? 22
Chapter Four: What Wasn't Said, Still Hurt 33
Chapter Five: Self-Medicating 44
Chapter Six: Rooted in Hurt, Reaching for Healing 54
Chapter Seven: Healing Seems Impossible 64
Chapter Eight: Sorting Through Emotions 73
Chapter Nine: A Mans Language With Love 78
Chapter Ten: The Heart of A Man 88
Conclusion: Bridging the Broken Places 98
About the Author 103

Introduction

As a woman who has shared many life experiences with men, I can honestly say—men tend to hide their emotions.

I've seen it firsthand. I have a biological father, had a stepfather, and I'm the mother of four sons. I've had relationships that taught me more than I expected, and I've interacted with countless men—whether the four fathers of my children, brothers, uncles, cousins, platonic, love interest, passing by on the street or sitting across from me in a professional setting. Across all of these moments and encounters, I've recognized a common thread: *guard your heart at all costs.*

Somewhere along the way, men were taught that showing emotion is a sign of weakness. They were taught to be strong, silent, and unmoved. They were told that tears make them vulnerable, and vulnerability makes them less of a man. They were taught to protect their hearts so fiercely that even those closest to them couldn't find a way in.

But I believe there is more to a man than silence and strength. I believe within each man is a tender, powerful, and honest heart—waiting for a safe space to be revealed. This book is my way of creating that space.

The Heart of a Man: Pure, Honest, and Unfiltered is not a critique. It's a conversation. It's a soft light cast on the shadows. It's an invitation to come close not to fix, but to understand. To witness the humanity, the pain, the resilience, and the beauty of a man's inner world.

As you read, may your heart stay open. May your perspective deepen. And may we all, men, and women alike, become better at making room for the truth that lives behind the eyes of every man.

— **Dr. Monica Beasley**

Chapter One

Where the Wound Begins

A man's heart is one of the most misunderstood and underestimated places in this world.

It is not cold or absent of feeling, as the world sometimes assumes. It is layered, complex, and often burdened with silent expectations. From a young age, boys are taught to toughen up, to stop crying, to be strong—not just physically, but emotionally. And so, a man learns to build walls where there should be windows. He learns to hold back tears that were meant to cleanse, and to carry pain that was never his to bear alone. But just because a man doesn't speak it, doesn't mean he doesn't feel it.

He feels disappointment, even if his face remains still. He feels heartbreak, even if he never utters a word. He feels pressure to succeed, to provide, to protect—yet may not have anyone protecting him. His heart often becomes a locked room where memories, traumas, dreams, and desires are stored, yet rarely visited. Inside every man's heart is a story—a journey full of moments that shaped him, silences that wounded him, and hopes that keep him moving forward.

This chapter begins the process of uncovering that heart, not to expose it, but to honor it. It invites you to look beyond the surface—to listen deeper, ask gently, and love without rushing answers. Because behind the stillness of a man is often a storm he learned to weather alone. And the truth is, even the strongest man longs to be seen, heard, and held—not just by others, but by himself. This is the beginning of that return. The return to the heart.

The first time a man gets his heart broken isn't always by a lover—it could be the absence of a father, the rejection of a mother, or a broken promise in childhood. That heartbreak becomes a blueprint etched into his soul. When he finally lays his heart on the line, trusting love to handle it gently, and it shatters—something inside him shifts. Every woman who comes after doesn't just meet the man; she meets the fragments. She touches the places where healing never fully took root. She gets the guarded smile, the measured vulnerability, the careful love—because his heart learned to protect itself, even if it costs him connection.

My first relationship with a man began before I took my first breath. My stepfather was already a part of my life, shaping my world from the start. From as early as I can remember, I could feel the quiet struggle within him. He carried himself as the head of the household, but behind that strength was a tension he never fully voiced. While he showed up, did his part, and helped raise us, I sensed that he often felt inadequate. Much of our financial support came from public assistance, and though it kept food on the table, it seemed to chip away at his sense of adulthood.

I won't make excuses for him, but during the 70s and 80s, welfare was often the only option for families like ours. Jobs were scarce, and pride had to be swallowed daily. The relationship between my mother and stepfather eventually strained beyond the bounds of love; they could barely tolerate each other. I believe that so much could have been salvaged through communication. If only my mother could have seen life through his eyes—and he through hers—things could have turned out different.

My relationship with step father was relational, formative, and foundational. He entered my life and left an imprint that still echoes in my understanding of adulthood. He was deep-rooted in love—his intentions were genuine—but I could always sense an internal tug-of-war between who he was and who he wanted to be.

He was raised in a time when masculinity was defined by hard work and financial provision. For a man like him, depending on welfare in the 70s and 80s felt like a betrayal of everything he had been taught. Work wasn't just a responsibility—it was identity, pride, and purpose. But the jobs weren't always there, and sometimes survival came at the cost of dignity. He never said it out loud, but I could tell it wounded him to watch his family rely on a system that made him feel powerless.

That unspoken frustration took a toll on his relationship with my mother. What began as a union filled with hope became strained under the weight of unmet expectations and emotional silence. Love faded into obligation, and communication all but disappeared. I often wonder how different things might have been if they had taken the time to understand each other's pain. Maybe if they had spoken more honestly, they could've bridged the gap that pride and hardship widened over the years.

Even with the emotional distance and financial struggles, his presence in my life left a deep imprint. He was the first example I had of what it means to carry both love and pressure in silence. Though flawed and often conflicted, his intentions were genuine. He showed me that men don't always speak their battles, but they feel them deeply. And even when a man can't give the world, his presence—his effort—still matters. His story became part of my foundation, shaping how I see adulthood, responsibility, and quiet resilience.

Even as a child, I could feel that tension in our home—the unspoken disappointment, the frustration of dreams deferred. He was present. He was involved. He helped raise us. And yet, I always believed that deep down, he wanted to do more. Not because he wasn't enough, but because the world had told him that being a man meant producing results, not simply offering love.

The relationship between him and my mother eventually became strained. What might have been love transformed into endurance. They tolerated each other, coexisted under the same roof, but the warmth was gone. Their conversations turned into arguments, and silence became their language. I often wonder: could things have been different if they had truly seen each other? If my mother had viewed life through his lens—a man feeling inadequate in a world that equated worth with work—and if he could have seen her resilience, her sacrifices, and the emotional toll of being the glue that held us all together?

This early experience shaped my perception of men. I learned early on that men don't always speak their pain; sometimes they wear it. They carry it in their silence, their distance, their sudden anger. I didn't know it then, but I was witnessing the emotional suppression society teaches men to embrace. And it stayed with me.

As I grew older, I began to see similar patterns in the men I dated, worked with, or simply observed in passing. Many of them had broken places they never talked about. Their first heartbreak—whether it came from abandonment, disappointment, or love lost—left them guarding their emotions like a vault. Every woman who came after was given only what was safe to give. Because once a man has been wounded deeply, he rarely risks laying his full heart on the line again.

My stepfather wasn't perfect, but he reflected so many men—carrying burdens quietly, loving imperfectly, trying to live up to a definition of maturity that was rarely forgiving. Looking back, I honor his struggle. I honor the role he played. And I understand now that even broken love can teach us something powerful.

It taught me that behind every hardened exterior is often a story of disappointment and unmet expectations. It taught me that adulthood is not measured solely by income, status, or strength, but by intention, effort, and the quiet courage it takes to keep showing up—even when it hurts. This early experience shaped my perception of men. I learned early on that men don't always speak their pain; sometimes they wear it. They carry it in their silence, their distance, their sudden anger. I didn't know it then, but I was witnessing the emotional suppression society teaches men to embrace. And it stayed with me.

But my biological father's absence told another story. He was mostly missing from my childhood and teenage years. I saw him sporadically—occasional visits scattered through time-like whispers. Life had kept him away, but it wasn't until we had a deep conversation years later that I discovered the truth: his absence wasn't entirely by force, but by choice.

He told me he had made the decision to stay away, though he had made attempts. He was living a fast life and had his own struggles. Still, he confessed something that pierced my soul—he wept over the years because I had become distant and cold toward him. How ironic, I thought, because that's exactly how I felt growing up without him—distant and cold, trying to understand why I didn't have the relationship I craved so deeply.

In that conversation, he shared his life experiences, and strangely, I could feel the weight of his journey as if I had lived it with him. Not having his little girl—me—present in his life was his first heartbreak. I can only imagine what it was like to maneuver through life knowing that somewhere out there, your child isn't calling, isn't texting, isn't reaching for you. And you have no one to blame but yourself.

At 48 years old, I spent my first Father's Day with him. After a lifetime of longing, it finally happened. I had craved his love for so long, and I know he had craved mine. Hearing about the circumstances of his youth and the losses he endured was heartbreaking. We're 20 years apart, but the pain and the desire to heal were mutual.

It took time to mend that broken relationship, but I'm glad I didn't let time rob us of that opportunity. I couldn't imagine losing him never having bonded. Love, even when late, still has the power to heal.

These two men—one who was there physically but emotionally distant, and the other who was emotionally missed and physically gone—shaped my earliest perceptions of adulthood. They taught me that men carry heartbreak too. Sometimes, it's their daughter's silence. Sometimes, it's the disappointment of not becoming who they hoped they'd be. But whatever it is, they carry it—quietly, deeply, and often alone.

I have four sons who grew up without their fathers, and I believe that is where it all began for them—heartbreak. It didn't come from a relationship, but from absence. From a longing that went unanswered. From a quiet, persistent question: *Why didn't he stay?* That question planted seeds of pain in their hearts that have taken root over the years.

What I've seen in them—what I continue to see in many men—is the silent war they fight with pride, insecurity, and jealousy. These are not simply emotions; they're burdens. They provoke reactions that often come out as anger, withdrawal, or defensiveness. All four of my sons wrestle with anger. It shows up in their relationships, their decisions, and sometimes, in their silence.

Having open conversations about emotions doesn't come easily for them. Society trained them—trained so many men—to believe vulnerability is weakness. That crying makes you soft. That saying *I'm hurt* is something you only whisper in the dark when no one's watching. So they bury their feelings deep beneath layers of toughness, humor, and distraction. But pain doesn't go away just because it's ignored—it waits.

Now, as grown men, I can see they craved a father's love. Not just someone who shares DNA with them, but a man who would show up. Someone who could model emotional presence, consistency, and strength wrapped in gentleness. They longed for conversations man to man, not from a place of criticism, but from a place of compassion. They needed someone to say, *"I see you, and it's okay to feel what you feel.*

As their mother, I'm grateful I've been able to create space for those deeper conversations. I encourage them to talk, to cry if they need to, to let the heaviness out of their hearts. I don't have all the answers, but I offer them safety. I listen. I remind them that healing is not just possible—it's necessary. Carrying unspoken pain only ensures that the cycle of emotional silence continues, passed from father to son like an invisible inheritance.

I'm ready for my sons to be free. To rewrite the story. To unlearn the lie that strength means silence. I want them to know it's okay to break down. It's okay to not be okay. Because men hurt too. And if a man's heart never finds a place to be heard, it continues to suffer in silence—longing, aching, breaking—while the world expects him to smile through it all.

Along the way, I've been in relationships where the father was absent, the mother may have been overly nurturing, or brokenness was simply evident. Looking back, it's clear those men were severely bruised by life. Some still haven't overcome the pain—they've learned to wear it, live with it, and call it normal. Life happened to them, and instead of healing, they adapted. Hurt became familiar, and survival became their response. They carried that unhealed baggage into every relationship, not realizing how much it shaped their actions, their silence, their trust issues. No one told them that the key wasn't pretending it didn't hurt—it was getting to the root. That's where healing begins. That's where the cycle can be broken.

Some wounds begin with love lost. A breakup, divorce, or betrayal leaves a man questioning his worth. When he has given his best, or what he thought was enough, and still ends up alone, it scars him in places that words can't reach. He may become emotionally distant or overly guarded, not because he wants to hurt others, but because he is protecting what remains of his heart. Rejection has a way of rewriting how a man sees himself, and many carry the silence of heartbreak like an invisible badge of failure.

Fathers being separated from their children is another deep wound rarely spoken about. Whether through broken relationships, court systems, or life circumstances, not being able to hold or raise their children leaves many men feeling powerless. They grieve birthdays missed, milestones unseen, and memories never made. Some mask the pain with anger, while others disappear into guilt. The ache of a father who can't father on his own terms is a grief that few utterly understand.

Prison changes a man—not just the time served, but what is lost in the process. Dreams are deferred. Opportunities vanish. The world keeps moving while he remains stuck in a system that rarely heals, only hardens. When he returns, society often greets him with labels, not grace. The shame of past choices and the struggle to rebuild can weigh heavily. Yet, behind the hardened exterior is often a man who simply needed a second chance before he ever got his first.

Addiction begins as escape and ends as bondage. Many men battling addiction are trying to silence deeper pain—childhood trauma, abandonment, depression, or unmet expectations. Whether it's alcohol, drugs, sex, or gambling, the substance is never the real problem—it's the symptom. Addiction is the mask worn by those who feel unworthy, forgotten, or too broken to be loved. Underneath it all is a man searching for peace but trapped in a cycle that numbs him instead of heals him.

Men raised without a mother or father face identity gaps that bleed into adulthood. Without a father, many boys grow into men lacking affirmation, guidance, or discipline. Without a mother, they may wrestle with emotional disconnect or feelings of abandonment. Some are raised by broken people and inherit broken tools. Grief for what was never present is real, and many men live with emotional absences they've never dared to name. That void becomes a wound they manage rather than mend.

Then there are wounds carved by life's harder truths—poverty, abuse, joblessness, violation, and the grind of hustling just to survive. Men who have been molested or violated often live in deep silence, shamed into secrecy. Those who hustle from a young age to put food on the table become men who never knew rest or stability. Unemployment or underemployment robs a man of his dignity. And for some, lust becomes both a comfort and a curse—filling the emptiness temporarily, only to leave them hollower than before. All of these experiences create fractures in the soul that, if left unhealed, turn into lifelong patterns of survival instead of purpose.

Chapter Two

The Effects of A Broken Man

When a man is broken—shattered by past trauma or heartbreak—he carries the weight of that pain into every relationship he encounters. The impact is deep, often invisible, and sometimes irreversible unless healing takes place. His heart, once full of potential and promise, becomes guarded, mistrustful, and in many cases, emotionally unavailable.

A broken man may seem functional on the outside—going to work, spending time with friends, engaging in daily routines—but inside, he is battling ghosts from the past. The heartbreak he experienced, whether from a lover, a parent, or life's disappointments, quietly shapes how he sees the world and those around him. He becomes lost, discouraged, and detached from the very people who love him the most.

Consider the man who ends a relationship with the mother of his children—not because she was abusive or neglectful, but because he simply cannot stand the sight of her anymore. Arguments, resentment, and emotional wounds create a toxic atmosphere. Unfortunately, his frustration with her begins to spill over into his role as a father. Instead of remaining connected to his children, he withdraws entirely, punishing them indirectly for the pain he associates with their mother. The love he once showed now fades into silence. The children suffer, confused and heartbroken, not realizing they're caught in the crossfire of a broken man's unresolved pain.

"I can't deal with her, and I'm tired of fighting," he says to his friends. But no one confronts him about the consequences of his absence in his children's lives. No one tells him, "Your children are not responsible for your pain. They still need you."

The way a man was raised by his mother plays a major role in how he navigates adult relationships. Some men, especially those raised in single-parent households, develop a deep emotional dependency on their mothers. That closeness can sometimes become toxic, especially when it delays his emotional maturity. A man who hasn't learned to "leave and cleave"—to detach respectfully from his mother and build an independent life with his partner—will struggle to maintain a healthy, balanced relationship.

His mother may not mean harm, but her interference becomes a quiet destroyer. She has a say in how he handles conflict, parenting, money—even his time. The woman in his life feels like a stranger in her own home, constantly trying to compete for a position that should already be hers.

"My mom said you were being disrespectful." "Your mom doesn't live here, and she shouldn't be involved in our personal disagreements." But instead of setting boundaries, the broken man lets the interference grow. And over time, love suffocates under the pressure of misaligned priorities.

When a man is not raised by his father, the absence leaves a wound that rarely heals on its own. He may not even acknowledge it. He may say, "I turned out fine," or "I didn't need him anyway." But deep down, there's a hole. That absence creates abandonment issues that often show up in adult relationships in the form of distrust, jealousy, and fear of rejection.

He wants to lead but doesn't know how. He wants to be loved but doesn't know how to receive it. He wants to stay, but he constantly feels the urge to run. He is living out a cycle of confusion and defense mechanisms—a cycle that only breaks when he confronts where he stands emotionally, spiritually, and mentally.

There is a dangerous pattern when a broken man gets involved with a broken woman. Instead of healing together, they often reinforce each other's wounds. She's been mistreated, so she expects mistreatment. He's been abandoned, so he expects betrayal. They become entangled in a relationship built on trauma, not trust. What should be nurturing becomes manipulative. What should be supportive becomes controlling. Respect fades, arguments rise, and love is smothered under unmet expectations and emotional immaturity. Instead of breaking the cycle, they keep feeding it.

The effects of a broken man aren't always loud or aggressive. Sometimes, they're silent and slow. He doesn't argue—he avoids. He doesn't yell—he withdraws. He doesn't cheat—he simply stops trying. He may love deeply but not know how to show it. He may long for peace but doesn't know how to create it.

He carries shame and guilt for the people he hurt along the way. He carries anger for the things he never received. And unless he is willing to dig deep, reflect, and seek healing, he will leave behind a trail of broken hearts, confused children, and relationships that never reached their full potential.

Healing is not a one-time event—it is a process. For a man to begin healing, he must first acknowledge that he is broken. That takes courage. It takes vulnerability. And it takes support.

He must be willing to sit in silence and reflect. He must forgive himself for past mistakes. He must open up, even when it's uncomfortable. He must be willing to see therapy not as weakness, but as strength. And if he believes in God, he must surrender his pain and allow the Creator to begin the restoration process from within. Only then can he reclaim what was lost—his peace, his joy, and his identity.

The effects of a broken man reach far beyond himself. They extend into families, communities, and generations. But so does his healing. When a man chooses to face his pain, he changes everything connected to him. He becomes a better father, a stronger partner, a more present friend, and a man who leads with love instead of wounds. The world needs more healed men—men who choose wholeness over hiding, responsibility over resentment, and purpose over pain.

Men are not always the ones at fault when a relationship begins to unravel. Often, emotional stress and pressure from a woman—whether through constant criticism, control, or emotional manipulation—can build up over time. While society frequently holds men solely accountable for relationship breakdowns, it's important to acknowledge that emotional strain can come from either partner. When a man feels emotionally cornered or unheard, the tension can reach a breaking point, and in unfortunate cases, the situation may even turn physical—something no one should condone, but that often stems from deep emotional mismanagement on both sides.

In many instances, the man tries to walk away. He wants peace. He desires space to process his emotions. But something—fear, obligation, or false hope—pulls him back in. He tells himself it will get better. He remembers the good moments and holds onto them, even when the bad ones begin to outweigh them. Over time, he becomes emotionally numb, staying in a toxic relationship far longer than he should. It is not always weakness that keeps him there—it can be a deep sense of loyalty or hope that change is still possible.

One of the most damaging things a man can do is jump from one relationship into another without healing in between. Each unresolved emotion, each unspoken word, and every unprocessed trauma follows him like invisible luggage. What hurt him in the last relationship continues to echo in his mind, making him suspicious, guarded, or overly reactive in the next. Without pausing to reflect and reset, he repeats the same patterns and experiences similar outcomes.

The emotional weight he carries doesn't just affect his romantic relationships—it leaks into his parenting, his friendships, and his ability to trust others. He might become controlling out of fear of being hurt again. He might shut down emotionally, unable to be fully present with someone who genuinely wants to love him. The women in his life may not understand why he keeps them at a distance, but he knows: he's trying to protect his broken pieces from being shattered again.

Healing is not only about letting go of pain—it's about facing it. A man must be brave enough to sit in his silence, acknowledge what went wrong, and ask himself what he needs to change. It's not about blaming every woman who hurt him; it's about taking responsibility for his healing and no longer allowing unhealed wounds to dictate his future.

Forgiveness—of himself and others—is a necessary part of that process.

Sometimes the woman he's with is not toxic, but she becomes a casualty of his unresolved pain. She may love him deeply, but she walks on eggshells, unsure of what will trigger him. He may not realize it, but he's keeping her at a distance not because she did something wrong, but because he hasn't found peace within himself. He fears vulnerability. He fears the past repeating itself.

Abuse in relationships is not limited to men as aggressors. While male abuse is often more visible and acknowledged, many men suffer silently from emotional, verbal, and even physical abuse by women. A man who is constantly belittled, controlled, insulted, or manipulated by his partner may begin to question his worth and withdraw emotionally. Because society often dismisses or even mocks male victims, many choose to endure in silence—afraid of judgment, disbelief, or appearing weak. Triggers such as emotional extortion, false accusations, or constant humiliation wear away at a man's sense of identity. Over time, he may shut down, lash out, or carry emotional scars into future relationships, never feeling safe enough to trust again.

Likewise, abusive behavior from men can stem from emotional wounds, identity confusion, or unhealed trauma—especially when a man is questioning or suppressing his sexual orientation. When a man struggles with same-sex attraction or is unsure of his orientation, he may internalize shame, fear, and guilt. To protect what society deems his "manhood," he may engage in relationships with women while emotionally distancing himself. This inner conflict can result in resentment or even mild hatred toward women, especially if he sees them as a threat to the image he's trying to maintain. Some men stay on the down-low—keeping same-sex relationships secret—while projecting control, aggression, or emotional coldness in their heterosexual relationships. This hidden tension can trigger abusive behavior as he battles between who he is and who he believes he's supposed to be.

The effects of abuse—whether from a man or a woman—are deeply damaging. The victim loses their voice, sense of safety, and confidence. Emotional abuse often lingers longer than physical wounds, shaping how they view themselves and others. Meanwhile, the abuser lives in a cycle of fear, regret, and emotional isolation. In cases where identity struggles contribute to the abuse, both partners suffer under the weight of dishonesty and repression. Abuse poisons the possibility of healthy love. Healing only begins when the truth is faced—when a man, or woman, confronts their wounds, acknowledges their identity without shame, and chooses growth over hiding. Abuse, regardless of its source or the pain beneath it, always leaves a scar—but honesty and healing can stop the bleeding.

A healed man doesn't need to dominate or defend constantly—he leads with peace, listens with intention, and loves with purpose. But getting to that point requires honesty, discipline, and the willingness to walk away from relationships that are more harmful than healing. It also requires courage to say, "I need help," and to seek therapy, counseling, or spiritual guidance.

At the end of the day, relationships reflect what we carry on the inside. A man who chooses to confront his emotional baggage instead of ignoring it becomes not only a better partner but a better version of himself. Healing is not weakness—it is power. And when a man decides to break free from the emotional burdens of his past, he unlocks the freedom to love without fear and live without regret.

In the journey of healing and emotional growth, a man must realize that ignoring pain does not make it disappear—it only delays its explosion. True strength is not found in silence or endurance, but in the willingness to confront what's been broken, to seek peace over pride, and to break generational cycles that no longer serve him. When a man chooses healing, he reclaims his voice, his purpose, and his power. And in doing so, he not only transforms his own life but also paves the way for healthier love, deeper connections, and a future built on truth—not trauma.

Chapter Three

What Anger Does to The Soul?

So much misplaced anger triggers unwelcomed affliction on others. When anger is not addressed at its root, it becomes a toxic wellspring, slowly corroding the essence of the soul. It leaks into how we think, how we speak, and how we engage with those we love. Anger, when left unchecked, becomes a heavy fog, distorting clarity and robbing us of inner peace.

Anger, especially when it stems from unhealed wounds, reshapes the soul's posture. It turns what was once open, compassionate, and trusting into something guarded, defensive, and suspicious. The soul, which longs to be free and expressive, becomes burdened with emotional debt. Anger becomes a prison where the bars are forged by painful memories and unspoken truths.

When a soul holds onto anger, it begins to lose its ability to feel deeply. Joy feels foreign. Love becomes complicated. Forgiveness feels unreachable. The heart hardens to protect itself, but in doing so, it shuts out the very things it was created to receive. The soul begins to mourn silently under the weight of what it was never meant to carry long term.

Anger can give the illusion of strength and control, but in reality, it exposes unresolved hurt. It causes people to lash out, to react before thinking, to reject before connecting. The soul, in its silent language, cries out for healing, but anger speaks louder — louder than wisdom, louder than reason, and sometimes louder than love.

One of the most damaging effects of anger on the soul is how it changes perception. A person ruled by anger begins to see everything and everyone through the lens of past pain. Even kind gestures may be viewed with suspicion. Words meant for healing are dismissed. Relationships suffer because the soul, cloaked in anger, anticipates betrayal more than it welcomes trust.

Spiritual disconnection often follows emotional unrest. Anger makes it difficult to pray, to meditate, or to rest in divine peace. It breeds pride, stubbornness, and the need to always be right. The soul becomes resistant to correction or reflection because it's too busy building walls. What was once a dwelling place of peace turns into a battlefield of internal chaos.

Anger also gives birth to bitterness. Over time, if not released, anger becomes resentment — a slow, silent killer of hope, faith, and dreams. The soul becomes numb, operating more in survival than purpose. People can be physically alive but emotionally and spiritually disengaged because anger robbed them of the ability to fully live.

Healing cannot reside in a soul occupied by unaddressed rage. Until the anger is named, processed, and laid at the altar of truth, the soul will continue to suffer. It is not until we allow God, or even trusted counsel, to walk with us through our anger that we begin to feel again — to love again — to breathe again. And in that release, the soul can be restored.

It seems like the men I have encountered carry a hidden aggression. Their demeanor is often condescending — dismissive, aloof, or hardened. But once time has allowed me to move past the exterior, I've come to see something deeper happening underneath. There is a quiet storm — unspoken pain, unresolved grief, or even a deeply rooted identity crisis. The anger they project is often not about the present moment, but about a history of disappointments and wounds they were never given the space or safety to address.

This anger, when ignored or left unchecked, morphs into something darker — something that doesn't just affect how they speak, but how they think, love, and exist. And because we are not living inside their minds, it is hard to fully grasp the depth of it. Yet, to those who observe closely, it is visible. I see it in the posture of my sons — how they suffer silently, how trauma has conditioned them to bottle everything up. Sometimes I ask myself, "Did something happen that I don't know about?" And while I may never get the answer, I can see what the silence has created — a soul in conflict.

Anger distorts perspective. It clouds the ability to see clearly. Instead of discerning truth, everything is filtered through pain. A kind word can be mistaken for sarcasm. A boundary can feel like rejection. The soul becomes reactive instead of reflective. Even blessings begin to look like burdens because the eyes of the heart have been dimmed by rage and mistrust.

Anger erodes peace. It keeps the soul in a state of unrest — always on edge, always anticipating the next wound. It interrupts sleep, pollutes thoughts, and creates emotional fatigue. The constant replaying of past offenses becomes a soundtrack of torment. True peace cannot dwell in a heart that won't release the offense because peace requires surrender.

Anger builds barriers. It convinces the soul that vulnerability is weakness. Walls are built — not just around the heart, but around conversations, emotions, and spiritual growth. Intimacy becomes impossible because nothing and no one is allowed in. These barriers may feel like protection, but in truth, they are a form of imprisonment.

Anger hinders forgiveness. It clings to offense like a badge of honor. Forgiveness is often seen as letting the offender off the hook, rather than freeing oneself. But without forgiveness, the soul stays shackled to the pain. Bitterness becomes a companion, and the mind stays trapped in a cycle of rehearsed arguments and imaginary vindication.

Anger feeds the ego but starves the spirit. It offers a temporary sense of control, even superiority — "I was wronged, and I will not forget." The ego thrives on that narrative. But the spirit, which longs for humility, connection, and healing, is starved of what it truly needs. The louder the ego gets, the quieter the spirit becomes.

Finally, anger delays healing. As long as anger is in control, healing takes a back seat. The soul cannot heal while it's still trying to justify its pain or demand restitution. Healing requires softness, a willingness to be honest, to grieve, to feel. But anger — especially in men — often disguises itself as strength, when in reality, it's a silent cry for help.

Men often attempt, figuratively, to conduct self-control — to suppress the anger, the tears, and the brokenness — as if doing so proves their strength. But what they consider strength can become unbearable to the women in their lives who are trying to love them through it. The women who see their pain try to offer comfort, but instead are often met with resistance, silence, or deflection. It's not that men don't want to be healed; it's that many don't know how to receive help without feeling like a failure.

That first heartbreak or traumatic experience becomes an imprint on their soul. It colors every future encounter. Even if love presents itself genuinely and consistently, their internal lens says, "This will end like the last one." The trauma whispers that everyone will eventually betray them. This distorted view convinces them they are protecting themselves when in fact they are isolating themselves from what could bring healing. The lie becomes louder than the truth, and even compassion feels like a threat.

Getting them to see the truth — that not everyone is out to hurt them — is one of the greatest challenges. You can show up with love in your hands and still be accused of having an agenda. When a man is deeply bruised and has not found his way out, it's like standing in front of a foggy mirror. He sees something, but not clearly. The wounds filter everything, and unless he chooses to begin peeling back the layers, no one else's voice, no matter how sincere, can penetrate his guarded heart.

Their minds become battlegrounds. Thoughts race — What if she leaves? What if she's lying? What if I'm not enough? The overthinking builds a wall, and that wall becomes their identity. Even in moments when no threat is present, they prepare for war. The emotional armor stays on, even during peace. And that makes intimacy hard. The women who try to love them often feel like they're hugging someone wrapped in barbed wire.

Yet, in small moments, you see glimpses of the man beneath the pain. A smile here. A laugh there. A softness that sneaks through when he lets his guard down — maybe when he's not paying attention or when he feels safe for a brief second. But those moments are often short-lived. He retreats again, remembering that to him, vulnerability equals danger. He fears being open because the last time he opened his heart, it shattered.

And so the seasons pass. Relationships rise and fall. New opportunities come and go. The women who love them grow weary. The children watching them learn to guard their own hearts too soon. And yet, the mindset remains. That inner vow to never be hurt again continues to hold them captive. It's not that they can't be free — it's that they haven't yet been convinced that freedom is safe.

I see the same homeless man walking up and down the street. It's been almost two and a half years since I first laid eyes on him. His clothes are always the same—this checkered black and red flannel shirt, brown corduroy-looking pants, and he always totes this big old garbage bag. His eyes are dingy and tired, yet there's something distinct about them. His hair is matted, as if it hasn't been combed in twenty years. But he walks with purpose, back and forth along the same stretch of pavement. One day, I was intrigued to stop him. I went into my purse and found a $20 instant lottery winning ticket. I offered it to him, and he took it—but looked at me as if I were the strange one. I began to wonder: what happened in the course of his life that led him here?

One minute I want to ask, and the next I want to respect where he is in his journey. Still, I can't help but think—no one becomes homeless without some type of trauma. Something life-altering must have taken place. A wound too deep to heal. A betrayal that shattered his sense of self. Maybe anger at the world, or at himself, left him emotionally stranded long before he ever lost a home. When I see him, I see more than a man without shelter—I see a story untold, pain unreleased, and a soul weighed down by regrets or moments that spun wildly out of control.

I bumped into him not too long ago. This time, I noticed his eyes were actually blue, piercing beneath the dirt and weariness. His teeth were crooked, and he had on a pair of green shoes—worn down so badly the inner sole flapped with every step. There were no laces. The shoes were rugged and dirty. I gave him $20 in cash this time, and out of curiosity, I asked, "How did you end up like this?" He looked at me and softly responded, "It's a long story." I gently asked if he'd mind sharing, and he said, "It may take a long time." I replied, "Then maybe there'll be another time." I didn't want to push him, but the question still echoes in my mind: what brought this man to such a state?

I often reflect on how anger, when left unchecked, can slowly unravel a person's life. Not all wounds are visible. Some men carry the weight of battles they never speak of. Sometimes their anger isn't loud or violent—it's quiet, buried deep, and expressed in self-neglect or withdrawal. It becomes a silent scream. He once loved someone. He lost everything in one crushing moment. He was let down by family, by the system, by life itself. Anger that doesn't heal turns into apathy. It convinces you that there's no use trying anymore.

I wonder how many people walked past him without seeing him. Not just physically seeing, but seeing his pain, his humanity, his story. Anger can dehumanize us—not just in the way we treat others, but in how we see ourselves. He might have been someone's son, someone's father, someone's lover. Now he's just the man on the corner to most. But to me, he's a reminder that every soul has a backstory. That brokenness doesn't always look angry—it can look quiet, forgotten, and exhausted.

Sometimes, I imagine what his life was like before the street. Did he once sit at a kitchen table, drinking coffee with dreams of his own? Did he laugh once without bitterness, hope without hesitation? Or did the anger start early—festering from childhood wounds, growing stronger each time he was disappointed, abandoned, or ignored? No one just arrives at the corner of despair. It's a journey—a long one. And if anger was part of that road, then we must recognize it as a powerful force that not only bruises relationships but can burn bridges to life itself.

Anger, when left unchecked, becomes a silent poison. It corrodes the soul from the inside out. It clouds judgment, severs relationships, and creates emotional distance even from those we love the most. But what many fail to realize is that anger is often a secondary emotion—it's the mask worn by deeper wounds like sadness, betrayal, fear, or rejection. To overcome anger, a man must be willing to look beyond the surface and discover what truly lies beneath.

One of the first steps in overcoming anger is acknowledging its presence without shame. Too many men have been taught that emotions equal weakness, so instead of facing their feelings, they suppress them until they explode. But healing begins when a man says, "I'm angry—and I want to understand why." Giving yourself permission to feel, without being ruled by those feelings, opens the door to real transformation.

Another powerful way to address anger is through honest communication. Bottling things up creates resentment, but expressing what you feel in a safe and constructive way brings clarity. Whether it's through counseling, journaling, or simply having a trusted friend to confide in, talking through emotions prevents them from festering. It takes courage to speak your truth, especially when that truth is rooted in pain—but silence only fuels the fire.

Spiritual grounding is also essential. Prayer, meditation, and connecting with God provide a sense of peace that anger cannot touch. When a man brings his frustrations before the Creator, he finds rest for his weary soul. God offers grace, clarity, and the reassurance that he doesn't have to carry his burdens alone. In divine presence, anger loses its grip, and healing can begin to take root.

Forgiveness is one of the most difficult, yet most liberating, tools in overcoming anger. Forgiving others doesn't mean excusing their actions—it means releasing yourself from the weight of the offense. And just as important, forgiving yourself is necessary too. Many men carry guilt for past mistakes, but redemption begins with self-compassion. When you let go of what hurt you, you create space for what can heal you.

Finally, overcoming anger requires daily commitment. It's not a one-time fix but a lifestyle of intentional emotional awareness. It means pausing before reacting, seeking understanding instead of control, and choosing peace over pride. With time, practice, and grace, the soul once darkened by rage can be renewed with patience, understanding, and love. Anger may visit, but it no longer has to stay.

Chapter Four

What Wasn't Said, Still Hurt

In most cases, men remember the bruises—the hurt, the lies, the untold story of *why* things had to happen to them. They replay moments of betrayal, abandonment, and failure like scenes from a movie no one else ever saw. But the ending is always the same: someone is still paying for that pain. A partner who loves them, children who need them, or friends who genuinely care. The wound they carry begins to leak into places it was never meant to reach.

The pain sticks like glue—thick, invisible, but heavy. It's hard to recover from something you've never really faced. And because many men were never taught to talk about their pain, they bury it. It becomes normal to suppress, to distract, to disengage. But unspoken pain is still active pain. It doesn't die; it waits. It shows up in their relationships, in their parenting, in how they manage disappointment, and in how they push people away the moment love gets too close.

There's fear in telling the truth—not just the fear of rejection, but of being misunderstood or seen as weak. Somewhere along the way, men were taught that expressing emotions made them less of a man. So instead of saying, *I'm hurt*, they lash out. Instead of saying, *I'm scared*, they withdraw. Instead of asking for help, they suffer in silence, navigating through life with a simmering anger and a hardened heart.

That anger is often misread. People think he's just short-tempered, rude, or closed off. But underneath that reaction is usually a memory that still stings. He was never affirmed by his father. He watched his mother be mistreated. He loved someone who shattered his trust. It's not always about what's happening now—sometimes it's about what never got healed then.

Men often hope someone will just *know* what they're going through. That someone will be patient enough to break through the walls. But emotional healing doesn't work like that. You can't be healed by someone guessing your pain—you have to speak it. What wasn't said is often what hurts the most. The apology that never came. The explanation that was never given. The comfort that was never offered. Those unsaid words echo the loudest in a man's heart.

If only men knew that speaking their truth doesn't make them weak—it makes them free. That healing doesn't start with pretending you're okay—it starts with admitting you're not. We can't keep asking the world to love our scars while refusing to show the wounds. What wasn't said still hurts, but what *can* be said might finally help set a man's heart free.

I've seen men walk away from situations not because they didn't care, but because they didn't know how to stay. The emotions they carried were too overwhelming to unpack, and silence became their shield. They weren't taught to lean into vulnerability, only to guard against it. So instead of asking for help or expressing pain, they disappear—physically, emotionally, or spiritually. And those left behind often carry the confusion of not knowing what went wrong.

Many times, it's not the loud moments that do the most damage, but the quiet ones. The absence of words when something should have been said. The lack of comfort during a time of need. The apology that never came. These unsaid things settle deep in the heart, where they begin to shape how we see ourselves and others. Men may not always cry in front of you, but that doesn't mean their soul isn't weeping in private.

I've learned that the things they wish they could say often get buried under years of disappointment. Some men don't even know where to begin. It's not always easy to say, "I'm hurting," or "I miss you," or "I wish things were different." Instead, they carry those thoughts like weights in their pockets—heavy but hidden. And when the pain becomes too much to carry, they act out in ways that confuse the people trying to love them.

There are men walking around with fractured hearts, silently screaming for connection but afraid of being misunderstood. Pride, fear, shame, and past rejection all build walls that are hard to tear down. Sometimes, what wasn't said was the very thing that could have healed a situation. A simple "I love you," or "I forgive you," or "You matter to me," could have changed the course of someone's life. But when those words go unspoken, they turn into barriers.

Not knowing how to express grief or disappointment leaves a man stuck in survival mode. He may learn how to provide, how to lead, how to show strength—but not how to release the ache that lives quietly inside. And so, pain becomes normal. Hurt becomes familiar. Distance becomes protection. But it's a lonely existence when no one truly sees the battles you fight in your mind and heart.

We must acknowledge that healing starts with truth—truth about what was lost, what was needed, and what was never said. And though we may never receive all the words we hoped for, we can still choose to speak healing into ourselves and into others. The silence of the past does not have to define the peace of our future. Sometimes the most powerful thing we can say is, "I no longer need you to apologize for me to heal."

Some men carry the burden of their first heartbreak like a lifelong scar. That moment—whether it happened in youth or adulthood—alters their perception of love. It's not just about the one who left; it's about what was lost inside of them when it happened. From that point on, love becomes more of a memory than a reality—something they once believed in but no longer trust. So they retreat. Not physically, always—but emotionally, spiritually, and mentally. They refuse to drop their guard, convinced that vulnerability leads only to disappointment.

Instead of allowing a new woman to love them fully, they create distance. Sometimes it's subtle—avoiding deep conversations, dodging commitment, keeping secrets. Other times it's loud—anger, cheating, pushing someone away just to feel in control again. They begin to see all women through the lens of the one who broke them. And when they encounter a woman with even the slightest similarity—be it tone, response, or posture—they convince themselves it's a warning sign to stay away, even when it isn't.

There are women who have stayed longer than they should have, hoping to love a man back to wholeness. These women carry the emotional weight of proof—believing that if they just love him hard enough, show up consistently, and stand through the storms, he'll finally feel safe enough to let her in. But when a man is still bleeding from an old wound, the love of a new woman can feel like pressure instead of peace. And in his inability to heal, he often misinterprets loyalty as manipulation or control.

Some men go from relationship to relationship, not because they want to hurt others, but because they are subconsciously searching for a reflection of something they lost within themselves. They are trying to find home again—a sense of belonging, of being accepted, of being safe. But without healing, this pursuit becomes harmful. It creates patterns of attachment and detachment, forming emotional bonds that are quickly severed when fear arises. It leaves behind a trail of confusion and broken trust for the women who tried to love them.

Without realizing it, the very hurt he once experienced becomes the hurt he now inflicts. He has become what wounded him. Not because he is cruel, but because he is lost in the cycle of unhealed pain. He tells himself he's protecting his heart, but in reality, he's projecting his past. He tells himself he's just not ready, but deep down he fears that no one will ever see him for who he really is—and stay.

Many of these men will admit to their pain only in pieces, if at all. It may slip out during a late-night conversation or surface in a moment of silence. But rarely do they allow themselves the space to grieve what they lost, to name what they felt, or to understand how it still affects them. Society hasn't made it safe for men to cry, to process, or to be vulnerable without judgment. So they mask their pain with ego, detachment, and distractions.

Healing doesn't begin when someone else fixes it, it begins when they choose to confront what broke them. It takes courage to unlearn toxic ideas about love, to let go of pride, and to admit that the pain still lingers. Some men are waiting for a safe place to fall apart, but they've never stayed long enough to see that love was never the enemy—unhealed wounds were.

True love isn't a threat—it's a mirror. It reflects back to a man what he still needs to address, and if he lets it, it becomes the beginning of restoration. But it takes a brave man to stop running, to stop hiding behind defense mechanisms, and to truly be seen. The words he never said, the emotions he never processed, the heartbreak he never healed—those are the keys to becoming whole again. And when he finds the strength to open that door, everything begins to change.

Somewhere deep inside, many men are still waiting to be chosen in a way that feels real. They've been overlooked, misunderstood, and mishandled for so long that genuine care feels foreign. When a woman comes along with good intentions, they often don't know how to receive her. She's not the enemy, but the wounded heart can't always tell the difference between danger and destiny. So he builds walls that she cannot climb, and in his silence, she begins to question her worth—when really, he's just trying to protect what little he has left of himself.

But healing asks us to do something radical—it asks us to face what we've been avoiding. For men, which might mean going back to that moment when everything shifted. That first heartbreak. That absent father. That broken promise. That time they felt unworthy, unseen, or betrayed. And not just revisit it, but feel it. Sit with it. Understand how it shaped the lens through which they now view life, love, and women.

What wasn't said is often louder than what was. The lack of apology. The absence of closure. The withheld affirmation. Those silent moments echo in the mind like a haunting melody. But the truth is, no one can rewrite the past. No matter how badly we want someone to make it right, healing isn't found in their words—it's found in our decision to no longer be imprisoned by them.

There is power in taking accountability for our own healing. Blame may feel justified, but it's not productive. Holding on to pain doesn't punish the one who caused it—it punishes the one who carries it. And far too many men are unknowingly punishing themselves and others for things they never had the tools to process. But once a man realizes he has the power to choose a different path, transformation begins.

Not every woman is out to hurt him. Not every act of kindness has a hidden motive. Not every "I love you" is a lie. But when someone's heart has been broken enough times, belief becomes hard. That's why grace is necessary—for both the man and the woman. Grace to unlearn. Grace to rebuild. Grace to take one step at a time without judgment for how long the process takes.

Letting love in after deep pain is an act of courage. It requires a man to peel back the layers of fear, ego, and survival tactics he's built to protect himself. It asks him to trust again, to try again, to believe that maybe—just maybe—love doesn't have to end in pain this time. And while it may be one of the hardest things he'll ever do, it is also the most liberating.

No man should carry the burden of brokenness alone. There are safe spaces, healing conversations, and people who genuinely care. But he has to want it. He has to reach for it. He has to make peace with what wasn't said, and decide that silence no longer gets to be the author of his story. The words he never heard, he must now speak over himself: "I am worthy. I am loved. I am not what happened to me."

When a man finally embraces healing, everything shifts. His posture. His choices. His relationships. He begins to love not from a place of survival, but from a place of truth. And what was once broken becomes something beautiful. The chapter may have started in pain, but it can end in purpose—if he chooses to say what was never said and become what he was always meant to be: whole.

One of the most healing things a man can do is put language to his pain. What wasn't said still hurts because it lingers in the mind without release. But when a man starts to speak or write about the things he's carried—disappointments, betrayals, regrets—he frees himself from the silence that has held him captive. You don't need to be a poet or a public speaker. You just need to be honest. "I felt abandoned when you left." "I needed you, and you weren't there." "I was hurting, and no one asked if I was okay." Speaking those words gives them shape—and once they have shape, they can be let go.

Often, what wasn't said to a man as a boy becomes the foundation of his insecurity. Words like "I'm proud of you," "You matter," or "I see you" were never spoken, so he grew up questioning his worth. One way to resolve this is by reparenting the wounded inner child. Speak to yourself now what you needed to hear then. Say it aloud: "You are worthy." "You didn't deserve that." "You are enough." These declarations begin to replace the silence with truth. What others failed to give you, you now have the power to give yourself.

Writing is another sacred tool. Grab a notebook and write the letters you never got to send—to a parent who was never present, to a partner who betrayed you, or even to yourself. You don't need to send them. You need to get them out. Use your words to release the pain, the anger, the confusion. Write without editing, without shame. Say what you couldn't say then. Let the paper absorb what your soul has been forced to carry.

Having open conversations with those who hurt you—if it's safe and appropriate—can also lead to healing. Sometimes closure doesn't come from the other person's apology, but from you finally speaking the truth out loud. Even if the conversation doesn't end in reconciliation, it can offer release.

The goal isn't to get them to understand. The goal is to set yourself free from what you never got to express.

Therapy or mentorship can be powerful pathways to find your voice. Speaking with someone trained to help you unpack your story can give you the language, safety, and perspective to say the hard things. Sometimes a man just needs one person to sit across from him and say, "Tell me what happened." In that space, with no judgment, the words that were buried begin to rise—and healing follows.

Lastly, understand that you owe it to yourself to stop silencing your truth. What wasn't said still hurts, but what you choose to say now can begin to heal. Say the things you were afraid to say. Say the things you wish someone had told you. Let your truth echo louder than the silence. Because when a man finds the courage to speak his pain, he also discovers the strength to write a new chapter—one filled with peace, purpose, and emotional freedom.

Chapter Five

Self-Medicating

Some men believe that if they numb the pain long enough, it will eventually disappear. But pain doesn't go away when it's silenced—it hides, waits, and resurfaces stronger. The alcohol, the weed, the pills, even excessive work, or sex—whatever the substance or behavior is—it becomes a crutch. It offers a temporary escape but delays the work of healing. What starts off as relief becomes dependence, and what was once manageable becomes uncontrollable.

You can't tell them to stop. You can't guilt them into changing. They have to come to that realization on their own. And sadly, some never do until they've lost everything meaningful—family, dignity, purpose, health. Substance abuse is deceptive like that—it promises peace but delivers chaos. It's not the substance that's the root problem, though. It's the brokenness that led them there. The pain. The trauma. The deep sense of inadequacy they've never learned how to face.

I've watched men I love deteriorate in front of my eyes—not physically all at once, but emotionally. Their joy, their laughter, their presence, all slowly replaced with silence, irritation, and unpredictability. They become hard to love not because they are unlovable, but because they are unreachable. Their highs are inconsistent, their lows are destructive. And you start to grieve them even while they're still alive.

Self-medication creates a false sense of control. It convinces a man he's managing his emotions when he's actually avoiding them. But the truth is, healing requires confrontation. Not of other people—but of yourself. What are you running from? Who hurt you? What lie did you believe about your worth? Those are the questions the bottle won't answer. Those are the truths a blunt won't help you process. You have to sit with yourself in the silence and ask, "What am I afraid to feel?"

Many men resist therapy because they see it as weakness. Society has conditioned them to believe that silence equals strength and asking for help is failure. But what if the strongest thing a man could do is admit he's hurting? What if vulnerability isn't the enemy—but the door to freedom? Too many men are trapped in cycles of self-sabotage because they were never taught how to be emotionally fluent. So, they drink instead of speaking. They smoke instead of praying. They shut down instead of opening up.

The stigma around men and mental health is killing generations silently. It's not just about what they're putting into their bodies—it's about what they're refusing to let out of their hearts. Suppressed emotions become toxic. They morph into anger, shame, depression, and relational damage. It's not enough to survive the day—you have to ask yourself if you're actually living, or just numbing.

Some of them know they have a problem but are too afraid to change. Others don't even recognize the problem because it has become their identity. They tell themselves "this is just how I am" or "I function better this way." But coping isn't the same as healing. And survival isn't the same as freedom. Real growth means stepping into discomfort and confronting the root, not just the symptom.

Watching this cycle play out generation after generation in my family has been painful. I've seen strong, gifted, compassionate men reduce themselves to shadows of who they could've been—all because they didn't have the tools to face their truth. They weren't evil. They weren't lazy. They were simply broken and no one taught them how to rebuild. Instead, they found comfort in chaos and escape in addiction.

You can love someone deeply and still not be able to save them. That's the hardest truth I've had to accept. You can speak life, show up, pray, encourage, and still watch them spiral. Because healing is a choice, and no matter how badly you want it for them, they have to want it for themselves. Sometimes, loving them means letting go of your need to fix them.

Self-medication often isolates men. They push people away to protect their dysfunction. They become suspicious of love, fearful of commitment, and hostile to accountability. It's heartbreaking to watch because deep down, many of them are kind, generous, and full of potential. But their addiction becomes a wall too tall for even the best intentions to climb. And slowly, they begin to believe that no one understands, no one cares, and no one can help.

But there is still hope. Healing is always possible. It doesn't matter how long the addiction has lasted or how deep the pain runs. When a man reaches his breaking point and finally turns inward with honesty, something begins to shift. The courage to ask for help is the first spark of transformation. The willingness to change is the seed of restoration. And in time—with grace, support, and truth—he can become someone he never imagined: whole, healed, and free.

No man was created to carry his pain alone. There is help, there is healing, and there is life beyond the bottle, beyond the smoke, beyond the mask. But it starts with a decision. A decision to stop running. A decision to stop hiding. A decision to believe that life can be more than survival. And when that day comes, everything can begin again.

There's a deep ache in a mother's heart when she knows her sons are struggling and yet feels helpless in guiding them out of their pain. I pray for them daily, not just for their protection, but for their minds and hearts to be made whole. I want them to see life through a different lens—not the one shaped by trauma or my past, but one that speaks of strength, faith, and self-worth. I want them to love with confidence, to lead with integrity, and to live without feeling like they have to constantly fight invisible battles.

Sometimes, I see the walls they've built—strong, guarded, emotionlessly on the outside. But I know those walls were built from hurt. Hurt that was never talked about. Hurt that was passed down, often silently. I wish I could go back in time and rewrite our story. I wish I could have shielded them from the moments when I wasn't emotionally present, when I was surviving rather than parenting with intention. But I can't change the past—I can only keep showing up now.

I often wonder if they know how much I carry them in my spirit. How much I want them to know they are more than what they've seen. That love isn't meant to wound, and maturity isn't defined by emotional distance. That being strong doesn't mean you never cry—it means you have the courage to heal. I hope they hear that in my voice when I say, "I love you." I hope they feel it when I pray over them silently.

Even if they don't say it, I know they have questions. Questions about love, trust, adulthood, and identity. And sometimes, I fear that my example taught them the wrong answers. That staying in relationships that devalued me taught them that dysfunction was normal. That seeing me tolerate disrespect made them believe that women are supposed to endure more than they deserve. But I'm speaking differently now. I'm moving differently now. And I pray that they are watching that, too.

I've come to realize that healing as a mother isn't just for me—it's for them, too. The more I repair what was broken in me, the more space I create for them to see something new. I may not have had all the tools back then, but I'm learning now. And I want to pass on something more than survival—I want to pass on wholeness. I want them to know it's okay to break cycles, even if it means walking alone for a while.

I watch them navigate life, and sometimes I see the same silent battles I used to fight. The look of disappointment they try to hide, the anger they don't express, the choices made out of fear or emptiness. I recognize the patterns because I lived them. And while I can't make every decision for them, I can continue to speak life into them. I can continue to be honest, even when it's uncomfortable. I can continue to love them even when it seems like they're pushing me away.

The hardest part is knowing they may not understand right now. That my attempts to correct what went wrong may feel too late or be ignored. But I hold onto hope that one day they'll see my heart for what it truly is—a mother who loved fiercely, even in her imperfection. A woman who made mistakes but refused to let them define the future. A voice that remained constant, even when everything else changed.

I don't blame them for their distance or their silence. I know they are still processing their own pain, trying to make sense of what they've inherited emotionally. And I also know that young men often struggle to express what they're feeling. The world doesn't always give them the space to be soft, to be confused, to be afraid. But as long as I have breath, I'll be a safe place for them to land.

My desire isn't to be seen as perfect—I just want to be seen as trying. Trying to be better. Trying to undo what trauma has written into our family story. Trying to equip my sons with the tools they were never handed. Trying to love them in a way that doesn't smother, but uplifts. In a way that doesn't enable but empowers. I want them to know they don't have to carry my mistakes as their burden.

I've come to believe that accountability is an act of love. It's not about blaming myself endlessly—it's about being honest enough to name where things went wrong, and brave enough to do something about it. I want my sons to see me as a woman who faced herself and chose growth. Who didn't let shame silence her. Who said, "Yes, I missed the mark—but I've found it now."

One day, I hope they'll look back and understand the weight I carried, not for pity but for perspective. That they'll remember the moments I showed up, even when I was empty. That they'll respect the fact that I never gave up on them, no matter how complicated things became. And, just maybe, it will inspire them to show up for their own children differently, with greater clarity and intention.

It is not okay to feel broken every day. And it's not okay to believe that brokenness is your final identity. I want them to know that healing is their birthright, not just mine. That love is still real. That life can be fulfilling. That peace is possible. And I will keep loving them, praying for them, and fighting for them with words, actions, and a heart that refuses to let them go—no matter how far they may drift.

No matter what they've seen, no matter what they carry, my love for my sons remains unshaken. It's a love that has grown through pain, matured through regret, and deepened through truth. I don't claim to have all the answers, but I do know this: the healing of a family often begins with the willingness of one person to change. And I have chosen to be that person—for myself and for them. They are worth every prayer, every tear, and every effort to break the cycles that once seemed unbreakable.

I can't go back and rewrite our history, but I can help shape their future. I can continue to plant seeds of wisdom, encouragement, and unconditional love. Even when they resist, even when they doubt, I will remain steadfast. Because I see their potential. I see the kings they are becoming. And I believe that one day, the love I've poured into them—flawed but genuine—will rise to the surface and help guide them toward their own healing.

So, I leave this chapter not with shame, but with hope. Hope that my transparency becomes their mirror. Hope that my growth becomes their permission to grow, too. And hope that love—real love—will continue to do what it always does when given room: restore, redeem, and reconnect. My heart is for them, always. And even when they don't understand now, one day they will.

Overcoming self-medication begins with acknowledging that your pain is valid, but numbing it won't heal it. Many men have turned to alcohol, drugs, sex, work, or other distractions—not out of weakness, but out of desperation to escape what they couldn't explain. The first act of strength is choosing to face the pain rather than suppress it. You are not weak for needing help—you are brave for wanting better.

Recovery starts with one honest moment. The day a man admits, "This isn't working anymore. I want peace, not escape," is the day his life begins to shift. You don't have to have it all figured out. You just have to be willing to take the first step. Whether it's through a support group, therapy, faith, or the help of a trusted friend, the road to healing is built one decision at a time. And every healthy decision adds power to your purpose.

Replacing destructive habits with healthy ones creates new patterns of thinking and living. Where you once turned to substances or unhealthy behaviors, you can now turn to fitness, creative outlets, journaling, spiritual growth, or community. These alternatives don't just distract you—they rebuild you. Each time you choose healing over harm, you prove to yourself that you are in control of your story.

Surrounding yourself with people who uplift, challenge, and support you is key. You don't have to overcome this alone. Lean into relationships that hold you accountable and remind you of your value. Isolation fuels addiction, but connection nurtures growth. Choose to walk with those who believe in your healing—even when you struggle to believe it yourself.

Forgive yourself for the time you spent in survival mode. You did what you knew how to do with the tools you had. But now, you're learning a new way. Give yourself grace in the process. Healing isn't linear—it comes with setbacks and wins. What matters most is that you keep showing up for yourself. Every time you choose healing, you're breaking cycles not just for you, but for generations to come.

Freedom from self-medication is not just possible—it's promised when you commit to the journey. You were never created to live numb. You were created to feel, to grow, to overcome, and to walk in power. Let today be the day you decide your story will not end in addiction—it will rise in redemption. And with every choice to heal, you're writing a future that's stronger, clearer, and filled with purpose.

Chapter Six

Rooted in Hurt, Reaching for Healing

Healing isn't an event—it's a process. And for many men, it's a process they've either delayed or denied for most of their lives. The truth is, beginning to heal often means facing everything you've spent years trying to forget. And that thought alone can be terrifying. So instead of digging deep, they bury the pain further, hoping time will do the work that only intentional reflection can do.

Some men have been hurting for so long they don't recognize the difference between functioning and thriving. They wake up, go to work, laugh with friends, even raise families—yet deep inside, something remains unsettled. A wound they've grown accustomed to carrying. A bruise they've trained themselves to ignore. Healing, to them, feels foreign. Unfamiliar. Even unsafe.

It's easier to stay where it's comfortable, even if it's painful. Growth requires a type of vulnerability that many men were never taught how to embrace. They've been conditioned to stay strong, keep quiet, and never let anyone see the cracks. But healing demands that those cracks be acknowledged, not hidden. It requires truth—raw, messy, painful truth.

There's no timeline for healing. Some men don't start the process until life forces them to—through heartbreak, illness, loss, or complete breakdown. Others begin quietly, in private, recognizing that the version of themselves they've been projecting is slowly killing who they really are. The longer they wait, the harder the climb. But it's never too late.

Healing often begins with confusion. Questions rise to the surface: *Why do I still carry this? Why did that moment affect me so deeply? Why can't I let this go?* These questions aren't signs of weakness—they are signs that the heart is stirring, the soul is seeking resolution. Men must learn that they are not wrong for feeling. They are not less than for needing time and space to unpack their story.

To heal is to remember—and that's where it gets heavy. You will remember the look in someone's eyes when they disappointed you. The sound of a door slamming when someone left. The words spoken in anger that you pretended didn't matter but echoed for years. Healing brings those moments to the surface, not to torment you, but to finally release the power they've had over you.

Some men struggle to begin healing because they feel they won't be believed or validated. They fear their story won't be understood. And so they suffer silently, letting decades pass without ever telling their truth. But truth kept inside will eventually turn to pressure, and that pressure will find an outlet—often in ways that damage relationships, careers, and self-worth.

It's not easy to admit that you're hurting. It's not easy to say, "I need help." But those are the words that often break the chains. It's in those small moments of honesty that the soul breathes for the first time. The bravest men aren't the ones who hide their pain—they're the ones who choose to face it, even when everything in them says, *stay numb, stay quiet, stay strong.*

Healing will feel like losing control before it feels like gaining clarity. Emotions may flood in all at once. Anger, sadness, grief, regret. It may feel overwhelming. But this is not destruction—it's release. All those things that were bottled up are finally being acknowledged. And only when you feel them can you finally begin to free them.

Many men believe healing is about forgetting, but healing is actually about *remembering without reliving.* It's being able to revisit a painful chapter in your life and no longer feel like you're still trapped in it. It's standing in your truth and saying, "Yes, that happened. Yes, it hurt. But it no longer controls me."

For some, the first step in healing is simply learning how to name their emotions. Anger isn't always just anger—it can be fear, disappointment, betrayal. When a man learns the language of his heart, he becomes empowered. He stops reacting and starts understanding. He stops blaming and starts releasing.

Healing is not linear. There will be days when it feels like progress, and days when it feels like you've taken ten steps back. That's normal. The journey to healing doesn't always look like strength—it looks like showing up, even when you're tired. It looks like telling the truth, even when your voice shakes.

Some of the deepest healing happens in solitude. In the quiet moments where no one is watching, and you finally allow yourself to feel it all. The memories. The shame. The longing. The broken dreams. Solitude can be sacred when you use it to reconnect with your true self—the version of you that existed before the pain.

Other times, healing happens in community. In safe spaces where you can be seen, heard, and affirmed. Spaces where you're not judged for your brokenness but honored for your bravery. Every man deserves a place where his story is safe, and where healing isn't just allowed—it's encouraged.

Forgiveness is a powerful part of healing, but it's often misunderstood. Forgiveness isn't about saying what happened was okay. It's about *you no longer having power over me*. It's reclaiming your energy, your peace, your future. Some men need to forgive others. Some need to forgive themselves.

Generational trauma often sits at the root of male pain. Fathers who never healed, grandfathers who never talked, cycles of silence passed down like heirlooms. But just because you inherited it doesn't mean you have to keep it. Healing gives you the power to break what once seemed unbreakable.

To reach for healing is to reach for wholeness. Not perfection—but peace. Not constant happiness—but understanding. A healed man still has scars, but those scars no longer bleed. They tell a story of what he overcame, not what still controls him.

The journey will test everything you thought you knew. It will stretch you. It will humble you. But on the other side, you will find clarity. You will find strength in softness. You will find confidence in honesty. And most of all, you will find yourself.

Men deserve to heal. Not for others, not for appearances, but for themselves. Because you are worth the effort it takes to become emotionally free. You are worthy of peace, of love, of joy that doesn't come with fear. You are worthy of a life where your past no longer whispers lies into your future.

Healing doesn't erase what happened. But it rewrites what's possible. And every man rooted in hurt still has the right to reach for healing. That stretch might be uncomfortable. It might be unfamiliar. But it is also sacred. And it is never too late to begin.

Some men wear silence like armor. It's not just that they don't talk; it's that silence has become their survival language. They've convinced themselves that staying quiet keeps them safe from judgment, shame, or vulnerability. The pain is there — buried deep — but behind the wall of "I'm fine" is a man trying not to fall apart. He shows up, works hard, and rarely complains. But under the weight of emotional silence, his soul often trembles.

A smile can be the most deceptive cover. Many men have mastered how to laugh through pain, crack jokes in moments of heaviness, and put on a brave face even when their hearts are shattered. The smile is a mask, a curtain drawn so no one sees the tears forming behind it. They've learned that showing pain might be perceived as weakness — so they keep pretending, even when pretending becomes exhausting.

Masculinity has been mis defined for generations. Strength has been twisted into stoicism, emotional expression seen as vulnerability, and vulnerability mistaken for weakness. From boys to men, they're often taught to endure without speaking, to grind without grieving. This chapter of life becomes a performance — pretending to have it all together — while the heart cries out behind closed doors.

Much of the internal turmoil stems from the unhealed echoes of a father's voice. Whether he was absent, overly critical, emotionally unavailable, or trying his best but still broken, the father wound lives on. Some men spend their lives trying not to become him. Others ache for his approval, even if he's long gone. But that ache — that invisible scar — continues to shape how they love, lead, and protect.

Anger is often the only emotion men feel safe expressing. It's not always rage toward others — sometimes it's frustration with themselves, their past, or a life that feels out of control. Anger becomes a familiar companion because it masks the deeper emotions: fear, rejection, grief, confusion. Many men don't even realize they're grieving because they've never been given permission to call their experience "loss."

Some men adopt the lone wolf mindset — distancing themselves from others not out of pride, but out of protection. Isolation feels safer than vulnerability. They don't want to be a burden. They don't want to appear weak. So they retreat, trying to manage their emotions alone. But even wolves get weary, and silence only amplifies the voices they try to drown.

To cope, many turn to numbing habits — alcohol, sex, work, entertainment, even church routines — just to keep from feeling too much. When healing feels overwhelming or impossible, distraction becomes their drug of choice. But eventually, the numbness wears off. The pain returns. And they're left wondering how long they can keep running from themselves.

There are men who are broken but still performing. They show up for family, lead businesses, serve their community — all while silently falling apart. These men wear strength like a suit, but inside, they feel hollow. They never admit it because they believe people need their strength. And in doing so, they rob themselves of the healing they desperately need.

Sometimes, the cry for help doesn't sound like words. It's in a changed tone. A missed call. A sigh that lasts longer than usual. The man might not say "I'm hurting," but his actions beg someone to notice. He might not know how to ask for help — or even if help exists — but somewhere deep inside, he hopes someone sees beyond the mask.

Healing doesn't start with having all the answers. It begins with truth. A truth whispered in private. A journal entry. A prayer. A hard conversation. It doesn't have to be dramatic — just honest. When a man admits he's tired of pretending, he opens the door for change. Healing isn't a straight path, but it begins the moment he allows someone in — even if that someone is himself.

Healing begins when you no longer allow pain to define who you are. Many men have been rooted in hurt for so long that they've forgotten what it means to feel joy, peace, or purpose. But healing is always possible, even for the deepest wounds. The first step is recognizing that you don't have to carry everything alone. You deserve rest. You deserve recovery. And you deserve to be whole—not just functioning.

One powerful way to begin healing is through self-awareness. Taking the time to reflect, journal, or speak your truth helps you identify the source of your pain. You cannot heal what you won't face. Ask yourself hard questions: Where did the hurt start? What patterns keep repeating? What do I truly need? These honest conversations with yourself become the foundation for lasting transformation.

Therapy or mentorship is not a sign of weakness—it's a wise investment in your future. Sitting with someone trained to guide you through emotional healing offers tools you never learned growing up. It gives you space to unpack, process, and rebuild. You deserve to be heard, seen, and supported as you evolve into a healed version of yourself.

Faith and spirituality are also powerful anchors in the healing process. When a man turns to God, prayer, or spiritual guidance, he finds peace that the world can't give, and pain can't take away. Healing doesn't mean forgetting—it means surrendering the weight of your past to the One who can carry it. You begin to understand that healing isn't just possible—it's promised when you trust in something greater than your wounds.

Creating healthy routines builds consistency in your life and promotes emotional strength. Whether it's waking up early to reflect, walking, working out, meditating, or simply being still in nature, routines help restore order where there once was chaos. These habits remind your body and mind that safety, stability, and growth are possible—and that healing is not a destination but a daily commitment.

Lastly, give yourself grace as you grow. Healing doesn't mean you'll never feel pain again—it means you've made peace with your past and chosen to move forward anyway. Celebrate your progress, even if it feels small. Each step, each boundary, each breakthrough is proof that you're no longer rooted in hurt, but reaching toward something greater—peace, wholeness, and the freedom to live without emotional chains.

Chapter Seven

Healing Seems Impossible

Oftentimes, men have a hard time breaking the barriers to start the healing process. They are glued to the past trauma — their minds constantly racing, unable to catch a breath to think straight or even sit in comfort. They need to uncover the mask and realize it takes time to heal, but once you hit that milestone of releasing what is no longer healthy to hold onto, you will start to feel better. Help comes from many sources. I have had conversations with men from different backgrounds who candidly shared issues that caused them to be guarded.

I met a gentleman who had been in sobriety for more than 10 years. He shared what life was like that led him to his addiction. He grew up around family members using, so that was the start. Both of his parents raised him, but they were addicts themselves. He said they grew up poor, and as a result, they were teased. He never finished high school, which he stated still makes him angry. Although he has been clean for a decade, he still faces internal struggles — insecurity being one of them. Men deal with pride, and that interferes with the healing process.

Some men are afraid of healing because it forces them to relive what they've worked so hard to forget. The thought of facing childhood wounds, betrayal, or failure feels like reopening a wound that never really healed. Instead of digging through the pain, they keep building walls, hoping time will make it all disappear. But pain left untreated becomes poison — and that poison leaks into every relationship, every decision, every part of who they are.

There's a quiet fear that if they start to heal, they'll lose the identity they've created to survive. For years, they've worn the mask of toughness, control, and indifference. But healing requires removing the mask and facing what's underneath. That can feel like stepping into unfamiliar territory — uncertain, raw, and exposed. Yet it's only in that rawness that the real man begins to emerge.

It's common for men to compare their pain, thinking, "Someone had it worse than me, so mine doesn't matter." This thinking delays the healing process. Pain isn't a competition. Each man's journey is unique, and each wound deserves attention. The moment a man gives himself permission to acknowledge his pain — regardless of how small or large it seems — is the moment healing becomes possible.

Some men don't believe they're worthy of healing. They think they've messed up too many times or hurt too many people. Guilt and shame become their shadow — following them into every room. But healing isn't about earning forgiveness from others alone — it's about learning to extend grace to yourself. When a man begins to understand that he is still worthy of love, growth, and redemption, something shifts.

The journey toward healing often starts with one brave decision — to talk. Whether it's with a friend, a counselor, a mentor, or a stranger at a recovery meeting, that first conversation can open a floodgate of truth. Words that were buried finally have space to breathe. The tears that were held back finally find release. And the man who once thought he was alone realizes that someone understands.

Healing is not linear. Some days feel like progress — others feel like relapse. There are moments of deep reflection followed by seasons of silence. That's okay. The goal isn't perfection. The goal is freedom. With every step, every moment of self-awareness, and every decision to break a cycle, a man chips away at the lies that kept him in bondage.

I've seen men who looked whole on the outside but were shattered within. Some wore success like a badge, while others hid behind service to others, thinking if they helped enough people, they could ignore their own pain. But healing requires turning inward, looking into the mirror, and facing the truth of who you are — and who you want to become.

Eventually, healing becomes a choice — a daily commitment. It means choosing peace over chaos, truth over denial, and vulnerability over pride. It's not an easy path, but it's a liberating one. And as men begin to walk it, they discover they are stronger than their past, bigger than their pain, and capable of becoming whole — one step at a time.

Healing feels unfamiliar — and unfamiliar often feels unsafe. That's why many men, even when offered a chance to heal, retreat to what is most familiar: silence, anger, isolation, addiction, or emotionally unavailable relationships. These coping mechanisms are not healthy, but they are predictable. And when a man is used to surviving instead of thriving, predictability can feel like comfort. The first step is recognizing that comfort isn't always a sign of peace — sometimes it's just a familiar cage.

Repeated offenses — betrayals, failures, or emotional wounds — can reinforce the idea that healing is pointless. Men often tell themselves, "What's the use in trying again?" But healing doesn't guarantee that life will stop hurting. It guarantees that you'll respond differently to the pain. The cycle of returning to what broke you doesn't stop until you make the conscious decision to stop feeding it. The patterns won't change if you don't choose to.

Many men fear starting over. Not because they can't — but because starting over means being honest about where they really are. It means saying, "I don't have it all together," and letting go of ego long enough to be human. Men need safe places to admit weakness without feeling ashamed. And they need to learn that seeking help isn't a sign of weakness — it's a bold declaration that they are ready for wholeness.

To stay on the path of healing, men must surround themselves with accountability. Whether it's a therapist, a mentor, a recovery group, or a trusted friend, healing happens faster when you don't walk alone. Accountability brings clarity. It calls you out and calls you higher. It reminds you of the man you're becoming when the man you were tries to show up again.

One of the most powerful things a man can do in his healing process is give himself grace. You will stumble. You will be tempted to run back to your old ways. But don't confuse setbacks with failure. Progress is still progressing, even if it's slow. The fact that you're aware of your cycles is already evidence that healing has started. Grace gives you room to grow — without the pressure to be perfect.

Lastly, healing takes commitment. It's not a one-time decision; it's a daily one. You will have to choose peace over pride, forgiveness over resentment, vulnerability over avoidance — repeatedly. The road won't always be clear, but you'll begin to notice something beautiful along the way: your heart getting lighter, your mind getting quieter, and your spirit finally resting. Healing isn't just possible — it's waiting for your "yes."

Self-Help Techniques to Begin the Healing Process

- **Journaling with Purpose:** Encourage men to write daily or weekly. Prompt them with questions like: What hurt me today? What do I wish I could say out loud? What part of me needs healing? Writing allows buried emotions to surface and helps identify patterns in behavior and thought.

- **Breathwork and Grounding Techniques:** Teach simple deep breathing (e.g., inhale for four, hold for four, exhale for 4). When anxiety or emotional overwhelm hits, this helps men calm their racing thoughts and refocus. Grounding methods like listing five things they see, four things they feel, three they hear, two they smell, and one they taste can bring their minds back to the present.

- **Replace Shame with Affirmation:** Many men live with silent shame. Introduce self-affirmations that directly challenge negative beliefs: I am worthy of healing. I don't have to carry this alone. My past does not define my future. Repeating these daily helps reshape their inner dialogue.

- **Set Micro Goals for Healing:** Big breakthroughs can feel overwhelming. Instead, encourage small, consistent goals — like reaching out to one trusted person, attending one support group, or making one healthier decision a day. Healing grows in the small wins.

- **Identify and Interrupt Triggers:** Men often react out of old wounds. Have them write down their emotional triggers (e.g., feeling ignored, being challenged, abandonment) and practice a response plan. This builds emotional awareness and accountability.

- **Create a Safe Circle:** Isolation kills healing. Encourage men to identify 1–3 people they can speak to honestly — whether that's a mentor, pastor, counselor, or friend. This circle can provide support, perspective, and encouragement when healing feels hard.

- **Practice Emotional Vocabulary:** Many men struggle to articulate how they feel. Offer a list of emotional words (e.g., rejected, frustrated, anxious, embarrassed, lonely) to help them label their emotions instead of defaulting to anger or silence. The more specific they can be, the more targeted their healing can become.

Healing can feel impossible when you're standing in the thick of your pain. The weight of trauma, broken trust, or years of emotional silence can make it hard to even imagine freedom. But just because healing feels far doesn't mean it's out of reach. Sometimes, the most important step is choosing to believe that healing is possible—even when you don't feel it yet. That belief becomes the spark that lights the way.

There will be days when your progress feels invisible—when triggers return, emotions overwhelm, or old habits creep in. But healing is not about perfection. It's about consistency. It's about waking up each day and deciding that you're worth the work. On the hard days, remember: feeling the pain is proof that you're alive and still moving. Numbness is the absence of healing; pain is the process of restoration.

What often feels impossible is really unfamiliar. If you've spent most of your life in survival mode, peace can feel foreign. If you've lived behind emotional walls, vulnerability can feel dangerous. But over time, with trust, safe relationships, and intentional effort, healing becomes more familiar than the hurt. You begin to recognize yourself again—not the version shaped by pain, but the man you were always meant to be.

You don't have to heal everything at once. Take it moment by moment. Celebrate the small wins—the times you chose to speak instead of shutting down, the time you paused instead of reacted, the time you reached out instead of isolating. These are not small steps; they are powerful victories. Healing isn't about getting it right every time. It's about refusing to give up.

Surrounding yourself with the right people is crucial. Healing thrives in environments where love is unconditional, truth is spoken with grace, and growth is supported. Find those spaces. Create them if you have to. Let people in who will remind you of your strength when you forget, and who will hold space for your healing without judgment.

So yes—healing seems impossible. But you are living proof that impossible things are possible. You've made it this far. You've endured. And now, you are being called not just to survive, but to rise. Healing is not beyond you. It is within you. You are not too broken to be made whole. You are not too far gone to come back. Keep walking. One step at a time. One day at a time. Healing is already happening.

Chapter Eight

Sorting Through Emotions

Many men have spent years disconnected from their emotions, not because they don't feel, but because they were never taught how to express what they feel. From an early age, boys are often told to toughen up, wipe their tears, and "be a man." But personal growth is not measured by how well you suppress your pain — it's revealed in how well you understand it.

Emotions are like signals on a dashboard. Ignoring them doesn't make the issue go away — it only delays the breakdown. When a man starts to feel overwhelmed, it's usually because emotions have been bottled up for too long. Anger, sadness, disappointment, and confusion can build silently until one moment tips the scale and everything pours out — often in unhealthy ways.

For many, anger is the first and only emotion that feels acceptable to show. It's bold, loud, and in some cases, respected. But underneath most anger is a softer emotion — fear, rejection, embarrassment, or grief. Sorting through emotions means learning how to dig beneath the surface and ask: *What am I really feeling?*

Some men fear being seen as weak if they open up. They worry that their vulnerability will be misunderstood or even used against them. But expressing emotion in a safe and healthy way is not weakness — it's wisdom. It means you are aware of your emotional state and no longer letting it control you behind the scenes.

It's not always easy to name what you feel. That's why developing emotional vocabulary is a powerful first step. Instead of saying, "I'm good" or "I'm mad," try being specific: *I'm disappointed, I feel overlooked, I'm anxious, I feel unworthy.* The more accurately you label the emotion, the easier it is to understand and manage it.

Men often suppress sadness because it's linked to pain they don't want to revisit. But unspoken grief doesn't disappear — it lingers. It shows up in relationships, work stress, poor health, and self-sabotage. Sorting through emotions includes allowing yourself space to grieve what was lost — whether that's childhood, trust, time, or a person.

Many men confuse vulnerability with emotional chaos. But being vulnerable doesn't mean falling apart. It means being honest — saying, *"I'm not okay,* or *I'm struggling right now.* It's a sign of maturity to be aware of your emotional state and seek support when needed.

Sometimes the hardest part isn't feeling the emotion — it's trusting that someone else will hold it gently. Past rejection or emotional neglect makes men hesitant to share again. But healing starts when you realize not everyone will hurt you. There are safe spaces. There are people who want to listen, not fix you.

Sorting through emotions also involves recognizing emotional triggers. These are moments that seem small but cause an intense reaction — often because they touch an old wound. Learning your triggers is part of taking ownership of your healing. Instead of lashing out, you pause, reflect, and ask yourself, *Where is this reaction coming from?*

Some men struggle with expressing joy, peace, or affection because they feel foreign or uncomfortable. They're so used to chaos or sadness that peace feels suspicious. But emotional health includes allowing yourself to feel the good just as much as the bad — to laugh deeply, to celebrate wins, and to accept love without guilt.

Relationships often suffer when emotions are not sorted. A man who doesn't understand what he feels will unintentionally confuse or hurt those who love him. Clarity begins inside. When you understand yourself, you communicate better, set healthier boundaries, and build trust with others.

Forgiveness is an emotional process that many men resist. It requires facing the depth of your hurt and choosing to release it. This doesn't mean forgetting or excusing, but letting go of the grip it has on your emotions. You cannot fully sort through your heart if it is full of resentment.

Sometimes emotions are stored in the body. Tension in your neck, headaches, back pain, or fatigue can be signs of emotional overload. Listen to your body. Learn to rest when you're tired, not just when you're burned out. Healing isn't just in the mind — it's physical too.

Men are often expected to "move on" quickly after emotional moments. But true emotional processing takes time. It's okay to sit with what you feel. You don't need to rush through sadness or quickly replace disappointment with distraction. Emotions are not interruptions — they are part of your story.

Sorting through emotions is a daily discipline. It takes practice to pause, name the feeling, and respond instead of reacting. Like building muscle, emotional strength grows with consistency. The more you engage your emotional life, the less power your emotions have over you.

Sometimes journaling is the safest way to begin. Writing helps you uncover things you didn't know were still buried. Putting your thoughts to paper brings clarity and helps you make sense of the emotional noise inside.

It's also helpful to have emotional checkpoints. Ask yourself throughout the day: *How am I feeling right now? What triggered me? What do I need?* These check-ins reduce emotional build-up and increase self-awareness.

Therapy, counseling, or faith-based mentorship can provide structure in sorting emotions. You don't have to do it alone. Sometimes you need a guide to help you unpack what you've been carrying for years. That doesn't make you weak — it makes you wise.

Faith can be a powerful anchor when sorting through difficult emotions. Prayer, meditation, and scripture can guide men to a place of peace when words fail. When you don't understand what you feel, God does. And He can bring clarity and healing beyond what you imagined.

Finally, give yourself permission to grow emotionally. You don't have to stay stuck in the patterns you learned. You can learn to love deeply, speak honestly, forgive fully, and live freely. Your emotions are not your enemy — they are the gateway to your true healing.

Chapter Nine

A Mans Language With Love

Men love differently than women. Their language of love may not always come in poetic words or daily affirmations, but it shows up in the quiet, intentional acts that often go unnoticed. While women are often vocal and expressive about their emotions, men tend to internalize theirs, communicating love more through presence than through poetry.

A man might not say "I love you" every day, but he'll warm your car on a cold morning, fix what's broken without being asked, or make sure you're safe walking through a parking lot. These actions are his way of saying, *You matter to me.* He may not verbalize his feelings with ease, but he demonstrates them with consistency.

For many men—especially those who have been hurt—love is risky. It requires vulnerability, and vulnerability often reminds them of rejection. A broken man might love deeply but remain guarded. He may say things he doesn't mean or pull away when he's afraid of losing control over his emotions. His love has been shaped by pain.

Sometimes, he says "I don't have feelings for you" while cooking your favorite meal. He may not show up with roses, but he shows up when your tire is flat or your day falls apart.

These contradictions confuse many women, but they make perfect sense in a heart that's still healing.

When a man is emotionally damaged, his love can feel inconsistent. One moment he's present and affectionate, the next he's distant and detached. This isn't always a sign of indifference—it's a reflection of his internal war between wanting to love and fearing being hurt.

Arguments can be a trigger for emotional expression. A man may lash out in frustration, only to follow it with "I love you" not as manipulation, but as a desperate attempt to hold on. He may not know how to de-escalate conflict in healthy ways, but his declaration of love is his way of saying, *Don't give up on me.*

Men often associate love with responsibility. If he's providing, protecting, or planning a future with you, that's his way of loving. He may not always verbalize his intentions, but his commitment often lies in what he builds and what he shows up for—not just what he says.

Touch is often a powerful communicator for men. A hug, a kiss on the forehead, a hand placed on your back—these moments are filled with meaning. Physical closeness becomes a language, especially when emotional language feels foreign.

Time and attention are a man's form of intimacy. If he carves out space in his busy world to be with you, even in silence, it speaks volumes. His presence is often his love letter, especially when he doesn't yet have the words to write one.

A man might buy gifts not because he's materialistic but because he wants to give you something he can control. When feelings feel unpredictable, a gift feels like a safe offering. He's saying, *"I don't know how to say it, but here's a piece of my heart.*

Sometimes men are misunderstood because they don't communicate like women. They might not journal their emotions or cry during a movie, but that doesn't mean they don't feel deeply. They just haven't been given the tools—or the permission—to express those feelings in healthy ways.

Many men equate love with problem-solving. If you share a struggle, he immediately tries to fix it. He's not dismissing your emotions; he's just wired to protect and provide solutions. It's his way of saying, *I hear you, and I want to help.*

Silence is also a form of expression. When a man grows quiet, it doesn't always mean disinterest. It can mean he's overwhelmed, introspective, or trying not to say something he'll regret. Silence is a space he uses to process emotion.

Broken men often believe they're unworthy of love. When someone truly sees them, it can scare them. They may act out or push away—not because they don't care, but because they're afraid of being truly known and then rejected.

If a man chooses to stay during difficult times, that's a loud expression of love. Staying when it's hard, when it's uncomfortable, when it feels like everything's falling apart—that's commitment. That's love in action, even when the words are few.

Men love through loyalty. He may not be as affectionate as you want, but he defends your name in rooms you'll never enter. He stands by you, even when you're at odds. That silent loyalty is love with a backbone.

Apologies might not come easy, but small gestures often say what words cannot. He may fix what he broke, bring you coffee the next morning, or sit in silence beside you. These are his peace offerings, saying, *I'm sorry,* the only way he knows how.

Sometimes a man's love doesn't show up until he's lost what he had. The grief of missing you reveals just how deeply he felt. Regret becomes his teacher, and in that absence, he learns the value of your presence.

Every man speaks a love language, even if it's not the one you're used to. For some, it's acts of service. For others, it's loyalty, protection, or provision. When you learn to see love through his lens, you realize he's been speaking all along—you just didn't know how to hear him.

A man's language with love isn't always fluent, but when nurtured, it becomes powerful. Give him space to grow, room to feel, and patience to learn a new way to love. When he feels safe, seen, and accepted, his love matures—and what once seemed confusing becomes beautifully clear.

Love for a man is often a silent vow. He may not speak it every day, but he carries it with him—like a mission he's determined to fulfill. He may not always get it right, but his heart is rarely absent. His love grows not just through romantic gestures but through consistent effort, protection, and presence that speaks louder than words.

There will be moments when his love feels hidden behind frustration, silence, or distance. In those times, remember: he may be learning how to show up emotionally while still carrying old emotional wounds. Healing doesn't happen overnight, and love—true love—often includes grace for the process, not just the outcome.

Understanding a man's love language means being willing to meet him where he is, not where you expect him to be. Just as women want to be heard, men want to be understood without judgment. The more we stop trying to change how he loves and start recognizing the love he's already offering, the more connected we become.

When a man feels emotionally safe, his capacity to love deepens. He opens up. He listens more. He gives more of himself because he no longer feels like he must guard his heart. That transformation doesn't come through pressure—it comes through patience, reassurance, and the consistent belief that his love matters.

Sometimes, the most powerful thing you can do is simply acknowledge his effort. Celebrate the way he loves, even when it's different from your own. Honor the small things, because those are often the bravest acts of love from a man who never learned how to say, I love you the way you wanted—but has been saying it in his own way all along.

A man's language with love is shaped by his past, but it can also be reshaped by the love he receives. When love is patient, kind, and understanding, it teaches him that he doesn't have to be perfect to be loved. And in return, he offers a love that is honest, raw, faithful—and entirely his own.

A man's love language is often subtle, quiet, and deeply embedded in action. While women are typically taught from a young age to express feelings, to share openly, and to value verbal affirmation, many men are taught to protect, to provide, and to remain emotionally composed. This difference in upbringing doesn't mean that men are incapable of giving or receiving love—it means they do it differently. A man may never say "I love you" daily, but he will make sure your gas tank is full, your doors are locked, and your needs are met. These gestures are not minor—they are his love in motion.

Often, a man's way of loving is mistaken as emotional distance. In truth, many men are emotionally present but express differently. He may not be physically expressive or verbal in a way that is familiar, but when he chooses to invest time, offer protection, share space, or stay consistent, he is showing love. He may not hold your hand in public but will work 60 hours a week, so your household is stable. If we measure love only by words or romance, we'll overlook the ways men quietly sacrifice for the ones they care about.

One of the most misunderstood aspects of a man's love language is his struggle with vulnerability. Some men have experienced betrayal, abandonment, or emotional neglect, and as a result, they build emotional armor. When a man keeps his heart guarded, it's not always because he doesn't care—it may be because he cares so deeply that he doesn't want to be hurt again. His silence is often a shield, not a wall. If he's still showing up—even imperfectly—that's love trying to break through.

It's important not to confuse a man's emotional caution with emotional incapacity. Many men have never been taught how to express or process emotions in healthy ways. That doesn't mean they're cold—it means they're learning. If you create a safe space where they feel respected, not judged, you'll begin to see the softer parts of them emerge. Love is not about perfection—it's about patience. Some men need time to translate what they feel into words or actions that others understand.

Physical touch, acts of service, words of affirmation, quality time, and gifts are all love languages, but how a man displays or receives them might look different than expected. For example, a man who craves respect may interpret a calm tone or appreciation for his hard work as affirmation. He may not care about gifts or affection as much as he values loyalty and peace in his home. For him, love may mean "I trust you," "I see you trying," or "I'm proud of you." When those needs are met, his capacity to give love grows.

Some men feel most loved when they are needed—not in a codependent way, but in a purpose-driven way. If he can fix something, protect someone, or offer a solution, he feels valuable. That contribution becomes his way of bonding. If he feels dismissed, unappreciated, or emasculated, he might shut down. Understanding this doesn't mean accepting unhealthy behavior—it means being aware of what helps love flow, not be blocked.

Receiving love can also be difficult for a man who has internalized the belief that he is not worthy of it. He may deflect compliments, minimize affection, or retreat when someone tries to get close. This is not arrogance—it's a wound. If all his life he was told to be strong, never cry, or always be in control, receiving love may feel foreign or even uncomfortable. Helping him receive love is less about telling him he's lovable and more about consistently showing it through presence, support, and kindness without expectation.

When men do begin to love, they love hard—often with a loyalty that runs deep. A man who feels emotionally safe will begin to express himself more freely. He'll initiate affection, open up about his fears, and show appreciation. But this usually comes after a foundation of trust has been built. Emotional safety is the soil where a man's love language begins to grow and flourish. You can't rush it, and you can't force it. You nurture it, water it, and stay close—even when the growth is slow.

Misunderstanding a man's love language often leads to unnecessary heartbreak. When his love doesn't look like the love you expect, you may falsely assume he doesn't care. But if you listen closely—not just with your ears but with your heart—you'll begin to understand his rhythm. You'll notice that love is in the details: the consistent texts, the protective gestures, the problem-solving, the quiet presence when you're not okay. These things may not look like love to everyone, but to him, they are sacred expressions.

It's time we stop asking, "Why doesn't he love like me?" and start asking, "How does he love, and how can I honor that?" Love isn't about shaping someone into your ideal version of affection—it's about seeing the real person and choosing to meet them in their authenticity. Men who love differently are not broken—they are simply built with another emotional blueprint. And when you learn to read it, you'll discover that their love is powerful, deep, and worthy of being received.

In the end, a man's way of loving may not always be loud, poetic, or easily understood, but it is real, intentional, and rooted in devotion. When we take the time to understand how he gives and receives love—through action, consistency, protection, and quiet strength—we stop misjudging his silence as absence and start honoring his heart as present. Love may look different through his eyes, but it's no less powerful. When we learn his language, we gain access to a deeper, richer, and more faithful kind of love—one that, though unspoken at times, is always felt.

Chapter Ten

The Heart of A Man

The heart of a man is layered. Behind his strength lies vulnerability. Behind his silence, fear. Behind his actions, untold emotion. Many men have been conditioned to believe that expressing feelings is a weakness, so instead of verbalizing their struggles, they channel them into their work, their roles, and their sacrifices. It's not that they don't feel; they just don't always know how to express what's buried inside.

Despite their flaws and imperfections, men often rise when it matters most. You'll find them pulling double shifts, fixing what's broken, and standing in the gap for their families. They may not have all the answers, but when duty calls, they show up. Their presence may be quiet, but their efforts speak volumes. It's in these moments we see the heart of a man beating loudly through his commitment.

Provision isn't just a task for men—it's tied to their sense of identity. When a man cannot provide, it weighs on him like failure, even when circumstances are out of his control. There's an invisible pressure that tells him to work harder, do more, and never show signs of struggle. Yet, what many don't see is that he's already giving his all.

Some men have risked their lives for the sake of their families. Whether in military service, dangerous jobs, or long-haul driving through the night, they put their safety on the line. Their courage is rarely broadcast, yet the reward they seek is simple: the security and well-being of those they love.

So often, men bleed in silence. They are expected to be the rock, the steady one, the unmoved. But that doesn't mean they don't ache inside. Many go through emotional turmoil without speaking a word, hiding it behind laughter or routine. While the world sees strength, inside they might be desperately trying to hold it together.

Family means everything to many men, even if they don't always say it aloud. They think constantly about their children's future, their spouse's needs, and how to build a better legacy. Some are building what they never had, trying to become what no one modeled for them. Their effort is their language of love.

Men often express love in unspoken ways. It might be through acts of service, financial support, or just showing up. A father's love may look like a quiet ride to school, a steady hand fixing a broken item, or a light left on during a late-night shift. These actions, though quiet, are deeply meaningful.

When brokenness hits, many men retreat. Not out of disregard but out of confusion and hurt. It's hard to fix what you can't name, and for many, processing emotions is unfamiliar territory. Anger, silence, or distance become coping tools in the absence of emotional tools.

Some men wear emotional masks so well that not even those closest to them can see the pain. They've been taught to be warriors—strong, stoic, and unshaken. Yet, inside, they may be battling insecurities, anxiety, or trauma. The war is internal, and it's often hidden behind a composed face.

Rejection leaves lasting scars. Even one moment of being told, "You're not enough," can shape a man's entire view of himself. That voice becomes a loop in his head, affecting how he sees his worth, his relationships, and his capacity to succeed. It takes more than success to silence those old lies.

Respect is vital to a man's heart. When he feels disrespected, it can deeply wound him. It's not about ego—it's about being valued, heard, and appreciated. A man will move mountains where he feels respected and shut down completely where he feels dismissed.

Many men have never heard the words, "I'm proud of you." So, they seek that affirmation through career achievements, status, or material gain. Yet, despite what they acquire, a part of them still yearns for that simple yet powerful validation.

Though they may not speak it, men are highly observant. They notice how they are treated and how others are treated. Their silence doesn't mean they're indifferent. Often, they are processing, assessing, and feeling deeply in ways they don't express verbally.

When a man falls in love, he commits with his whole being. It may not be poetic or dramatic, but it is unwavering. His love is shown through consistency, responsibility, and loyalty. When that love is betrayed or dismissed, it cuts him deeply, changing him forever.

Being a man in today's world comes with invisible weight. He's expected to be strong but sensitive, successful but humble, stoic but emotionally available. These contradicting expectations can create inner tension that feels overwhelming.

Grief looks different for men. Some carry the loss of loved ones or dreams quietly. They may not cry or talk about it, but their grief shows in their distance, their silence, or their overworking. The mourning is there—it's just hidden.

Coping can take many forms—some healthy, some not. When men don't have an outlet, they may turn to addiction, overworking, or emotional detachment. These responses aren't about not caring—they're about trying to survive pain they don't yet understand.

The phrase "man up" has created emotional suppression in boys that grows into adulthood. It teaches them to hide their tears, to ignore pain, and to disconnect from their emotional selves. Undoing this mindset takes time, patience, and a safe environment to feel.

Every man carries a younger version of himself within. The boy who wanted to be held, affirmed, or seen. That boy often surfaces when he feels unsafe or misunderstood, and healing often means tending to that little boy's wounds with compassion.

Silence, for many men, is a shield. It doesn't mean they don't care—it means they're protecting others from their internal storms. It means they don't want to be a burden or don't believe anyone will understand what they're going through.

To be vulnerable is one of the most courageous acts a man can perform. Admitting pain, confessing fears, or asking for help goes against everything society has conditioned him to be. Yet, vulnerability is where true healing begins.

Some men didn't grow up seeing healthy love. They witnessed abandonment, conflict, or manipulation. So when they try to love, they are doing so without a map. Still, many are learning, unlearning, and choosing to give something better to their families.

Purpose drives a man. He wants to be useful, to make an impact. When he feels aimless, depression can sneak in. He may still function, but inside, he feels adrift—longing for meaning. Beneath the surface, many men are battling intense pressures: financial burdens, self-doubt, past trauma, and the fear of failing those they love. These internal battles are fought with a straight face, a steady hand, and often, without support.

People rarely ask a man how he's really doing. His strength is often assumed. But behind the smiles and nods, he could be holding back tears. Men deserve the same grace and check-ins they so often offer others. Spirituality can be a lifeline. When a man leans on God, on faith, or on a higher calling, he finds strength that surpasses his own. It's in surrender that he often discovers resilience and peace.

Men need safe spaces—places where they don't have to perform or pretend. Spaces where they can feel, speak, cry, and simply be. These environments allow men to exhale and be human. Becoming a father often unlocks new parts of a man's heart. He becomes softer, more protective, and more aware. The responsibility may feel heavy, but the love that grows is transformative.

Even the most broken man can be restored. Redemption isn't reserved for the perfect—it's for the willing. With love, support, and grace, he can rebuild himself and rewrite his story. When nurtured, the heart of a man is deeply compassionate, wise, and loyal. He becomes a source of strength and love, not because he's perfect, but because he is present, authentic, and trying.

The heart of a man is both resilient and fragile. It's capable of deep love, unshakable loyalty, and enduring patience. Yet, it is also one of the most misunderstood and mistreated parts of who he is. While many see his strength and assume he can carry anything, few recognize the emotional weight he quietly endures. Some men have carried the emotional baggage of others for years, especially from relationships with women who are bitter, manipulative, or emotionally wounded themselves.

There are men who stay in relationships with ungrateful women—not because they are weak, but because they are committed. They give their best: their time, effort, income, faithfulness, and support, yet it never is enough. These men suffer in silence, working hard to hold together what feels like a one-sided relationship. They don't always complain, but they feel the emotional starvation when their efforts are unappreciated, and their love is met with indifference or entitlement. Still, they stay. Not for reward, but out of principle—because they made a promise, and they intend to keep it.

Manipulation cuts deeper than most wounds because it comes wrapped in affection. Some women use a man's love as leverage—shaping his actions through guilt, passive aggression, or emotional punishment. These tactics confuse a man who is genuinely trying to show up. He may begin to question himself, to wonder if his love is wrong or if he's doing too much. Over time, he may grow emotionally numb, not because he doesn't care, but because he's trying to protect what's left of his dignity and peace.

There are also women who come into relationships not to build, but to dominate. Overbearing attitudes, constant criticism, or dismissive behaviors chip away at a man's confidence. He may feel emasculated in his own home, his voice silenced, his leadership questioned. Still, many men endure—not because they lack options, but because they value family, they don't want to abandon their children, or they're hoping for healing to happen. Tolerating disrespect doesn't mean they don't recognize it—it means they're holding on longer than they should, believing in the possibility of change.

And then there's deception. A man can give his all to a woman who wears a mask. She pretends to love, pretends to be loyal, pretends to support him—until the truth comes out. The betrayal stings not just because of the lie, but because of the effort he put in while believing it was real. He loved purely, and sometimes that wasn't enough. When a man gives his whole heart and is met with manipulation or deceit, he begins to question his judgment, his worth, and his ability to ever trust again.

Despite all this, many men still choose to lead with love. They strive to understand what a healthy relationship requires. They read, they pray, they go to counseling, they ask questions. They humble themselves. They try to fix what they didn't break because they want peace more than they want to be right. A good man will do what it takes to build something meaningful—even with a partner who doesn't make it easy. His heart longs for connection, for appreciation, for a safe space to be both strong and soft.

When he's met with resistance, bitterness, or indifference, he doesn't always walk away. He may pause. He may withdraw. But deep down, he's still hoping. He's still trying. He's still asking, "What more can I do?" And sometimes the heartbreak lies in knowing he has done all he can, but his effort is mistaken for weakness. He gets labeled as passive, as inattentive, or even as cold—but those labels ignore the silent work he's been doing all along.

The truth is that a man's heart was never designed to tolerate emotional abuse. His strength doesn't excuse the damage done by unhealed partners. He deserves respect just as much as he gives it. He needs love just as much as he offers it. And when a man reaches the point where he realizes that love without respect is unsustainable, he begins to value his peace more than proximity. That's when he either withdraws emotionally—or walks away physically.

Yet even in the midst of dysfunction, many men still choose to operate from a place of integrity. They stay present for their children. They continue to provide. They pray through the pain. They encourage their partners even when they aren't being encouraged. This quiet endurance is often overlooked, but it is noble. It is not weakness—it is discipline. And while many men are hurting, they continue to hope. Hope for better communication. Hope for emotional safety. Hope for a relationship that feeds them as much as they pour out.

The heart of a man is powerful—not just because of how much he can endure, but because of how deeply he still chooses to love. He may be tired. He may be disappointed. But when he loves, he loves with the hope that something real can grow. He's not asking for perfection—only honesty, effort, peace, and partnership. And when a woman sees and honors his heart, she unlocks a version of him that no one else will ever know: loyal, consistent, fully present, and deeply committed.

Conclusion

Bridging the Broken Places

Throughout this journey, we have unwrapped the many layers of a man's heart—the silent ache, the untold stories, the emotional voids, and the quiet battles waged beneath the surface. From the opening chapter, *Where the Wound Begins*, we saw that pain doesn't arrive without a source. Whether it's the absence of a father, a mother's silent struggles, or childhood trauma never addressed, many wounds trace back to places where a boy was forced to grow before he was ready.

By Chapter Two, *What Anger Does to the Soul*, we came face-to-face with one of the most misunderstood emotions. Anger, especially in men, is often misinterpreted as aggression or coldness. But in reality, it's often unprocessed grief, fear, shame, or abandonment. It becomes a shield, guarding their most vulnerable places. The soul of a man, bruised and burdened, begins to speak through anger when no other language feels safe. This form of expression, while harmful to others and himself, often stems from an unresolved wound that has festered in the dark.

In *What Wasn't Said, Still Hurt*, we recognized that silence can be just as damaging as harsh words. The words never spoken— "I'm proud of you," "I love you," "You didn't deserve that"—echo louder than anything ever said. Men, taught to suppress emotions, carry these unsaid truths deep in their chest. They move through life building barriers, believing that their emotions are weaknesses to be hidden. And yet, those unspoken experiences form the foundation for broken relationships, emotional disconnection, and self-doubt.

Chapter Four revealed how many men turn to *Self-Medication* as a coping mechanism. Whether through substances, overworking, emotional detachment, or meaningless relationships, these choices numb pain they can't name. The man who drinks excessively or constantly runs from commitment isn't always careless—he's trying to escape a prison built by emotional neglect, broken trust, or generational pain. Addiction isn't the root—it's the fruit of what's been buried far too long.

But we turned a hopeful corner in Chapter Five: *Rooted in Hurt, Reaching for Healing.* We explored the truth that healing is not a destination but a process—one that begins when a man no longer wants to stay the same. It takes courage to reach back into the past and name the source of pain. Some will resist this path for years. Others will embrace it when life finally forces them to choose between growth and continued suffering. But once a man decides to heal, everything around him begins to change—his relationships, his confidence, and his legacy.

Still, healing is not easy. In Chapter Six: *Healing Seems Impossible*, we acknowledged the challenges that come with change. Emotional triggers, unresolved trauma, and fear of vulnerability can make healing feel unreachable. Some men relapse emotionally, returning to what is familiar because it feels safer than the unknown. But healing does not happen in a straight line. It's messy, uncomfortable, and deeply personal. The key is to keep moving forward, even if it's just one step at a time.

As we began *Sorting Through Emotions* in Chapter Seven, we saw the importance of teaching men emotional literacy. Many men don't know the difference between sadness and depression, anger and hurt, fear and failure. Giving them permission—and the tools—to feel, to cry, to express without shame is essential. Emotions are not the enemy; they are indicators, calling attention to something deeper. When a man learns how to navigate his emotions, he becomes more aware, more connected, and more capable of sustaining meaningful relationships.

In Chapter Eight, *A Man's Language With Love*, we explored the truth that men love differently. Their expressions of affection may come in actions rather than words—in silent support, in thoughtful gestures, in simply staying. A man may not always say "I love you," but he will make sure you're safe, that your needs are met, and that you're cared for. Often, brokenness masks these expressions. Pain distorts communication. But beneath the layers, men have an incredible capacity to love with loyalty, tenderness, and devotion when they feel emotionally safe.

Finally, in *The Heart of A Man*, we looked into the core of his being. His heart carries responsibility, pressure, purpose, and passion. Often unappreciated, the heart of a man still shows up—at work, at home, in relationships—doing the best it can with what it was given. The heart of a man, when nurtured and understood, is a powerful force. It becomes a vessel of strength, compassion, and leadership. But when neglected, it becomes a quiet battlefield where shame and silence wage war.

These chapters are more than just reflections—they are revelations. They tell the story of men who are more than their mistakes. Men who are not emotionless, but simply misunderstood. Men who have the ability to heal, grow, and love deeply if given the right environment.

This book is an invitation—to women, to sons, to fathers, to partners, to communities—to take a second look at the men in their lives. To listen for what's not being said. To extend grace in place of judgment. To create spaces where vulnerability is not penalized, but honored.

To the men reading this: You are not alone in your pain. You are not weak for feeling. You are not broken beyond repair. There is hope for your heart. There is healing for your soul. And there is love that can meet you right where you are.

May this be the beginning of your transformation, not the end of your story. Let the chapters of your life from this point forward be written with clarity, courage, healing, and the truth that **you are worthy of being whole**.

About the Author

Dr. Monica Denise Beasley is a transformative leader, serial author, and respected voice in both ministry and business. She is the President and founder of **Monica's Accounting & Tax Service (MATS LLC)**, a thriving firm based in Champaign, Illinois, where she provides expert tax preparation, accounting, payroll, business startup consulting, and nonprofit formation services to individuals, small businesses, and community organizations. Her firm reflects her unwavering commitment to economic empowerment, financial literacy, and generational stability.

In addition to her business acumen, Dr. Beasley is a prolific author and inspirational figure. Her debut memoir, *Look What God Has Done for Me: The Epitome of Monica*, details her powerful journey through hardship, redemption, and the undeniable hand of God. In *Journaling Became My Second Guide: My Story of Healing, Purpose, and God's Faithful Promises*, she invites readers into a deeply personal process of emotional restoration and spiritual growth through the written word. Her most recent book, *Soul Mate: A Hidden Treasure*, explores the divine design for love, timing, and spiritual alignment in relationships.

Dr. Beasley holds an **Associate of Applied Science (AAS) in Accounting**, a **Bachelor of Science in Business**

Administration, Master of Science degrees in both **Human Resource Management** and **Accounting & Financial Management**, and a **Doctor of Philosophy (Ph.D.) in Business Administration**. Her education is matched by more than two decades of professional experience in leadership, ministry, and mentoring. Her academic and life credentials make her uniquely equipped to speak into the intersection of emotional healing, financial independence, and spiritual breakthrough.

She is also the President of **Open Arms Graces**, a nonprofit initiative committed to serving low-income families through advocacy, education, and emotional support. Her outreach work reflects her heart for people, especially those overcoming trauma, poverty, incarceration, and spiritual confusion. Dr. Beasley mentors men and women through life's most painful seasons—helping them reclaim hope and build meaningful, purpose-driven lives.

As a mother of seven, speaker, musician, and visionary, Dr. Monica Denise Beasley is a true example of resilience and restoration. Her transparency, compassion, and faith-infused guidance have touched lives across the country. Whether in the boardroom, the pulpit, or the pages of her books, Dr. Beasley's message is clear: your pain is not your ending, and healing is possible for anyone who dares to believe again.

Made in the USA
Monee, IL
28 June 2025